D1613005

ST. HELENS ~~~~~~ COUNCIL
LOCAL ~~~~~~ ~~RY

D 52 Fu.

NOT TO BE TAKEN AWAY

VAMP TILL READY

Further Memoirs

ROY FULLER

my troth is plighted
with guilty classes sure to be defeated.
— Drummond Allison: "For Karl Marx"

82/35665

London Magazine Editions

1982

By the Same Author

Souvenirs (memoirs)

The Reign of Sparrows (poems)

ST. HELENS PUBLIC LIBRARIES

The publishers acknowledge the financial assistance of the
Arts Council

Published by London Magazine Editions
30 Thurloe Place, London SW7
© Roy Fuller
SBN 904388 45 X

Printed by Unwin Brothers Limited,
The Gresham Press,
Old Woking, Surrey

Contents

1 Dixie

One's memory works both ways.

— Through the Looking Glass

If not so desperately as to re-live life, one longs to re-write auto-biography. In *Souvenirs*, a memoir of my childhood and youth, I called one chapter "Happy Valley", the name given to a sunken piece of land in Blackpool where once upon a time mediocre pierrots performed in the open air. It was familiar to me and to my wife when we were very young, though not coming to know each other until our late teens. A fair ignoramus, I did not read *Rasselas* until after January 1939, the date I wrote on the fly-leaf of my second-hand copy at the time. Did the book bring to mind the real place I had known? Doubtful: childhood and Blackpool were things I wouldn't in the least want to dwell on as a married man of twenty-six, successfully escaped from the provinces. But less than nine months after I inscribed that date, my wife and son, driven from London by the threat of bombing, were living in exile in her parents' house overlooking the occidental Happy Valley, cognomen then ironic indeed. Moreover, the only entertainments it had come to offer were putting, and sitting on benches below the municipal rockery.

The music of the vanished pierrots played a part in our puerile aesthetic lives, so had I brought to mind the *Rasselas* connection I might very well have used as an epigraph for that chapter of *Souvenirs* these words from Dr Johnson's tale: "They were daily entertained with songs, the subject of which was the Happy Valley." The regret for the omission is not just that of an incurably literary mind: the quotation and its attendant circumstances would have

1

neatly and aptly, if trivially, demonstrated the changes made to the past by time and knowledge. Somewhat amazing, incidentally, not quite that Johnson's name for his Abyssinian locale should have entered general consciousness but that it should have survived until sufficiently vulgar modern times.

Of course, those songs sung in our seedtime were not about Happy Valley itself: however, despite their quota of nostalgia and melancholy, they often concerned the ideal life:

> What a welcome there will be
> When you say that you know me!
> Daddy's eyes will shine, he'll say "Fine —
> If you're a friend of his, then you're a friend of mine."

The singer is not able himself to go back to his family in Dixie, but the person addressed is about to make the journey and is being assured of a warm-hearted reception. I quote from memory but have not distorted the sentiment, which is typical of the period. There is no hint that the son's (or possibly daughter's) continuing absence is in any way undutiful, let alone that the friend is a scrounger or that his visit will be an unwelcome imposition.

Perhaps my whole life could be depicted in terms of the destruction or modification of public and private illusions. Though I cannot say that a rose-coloured view of parental homes was ever an article of faith with me (and certainly the return to Happy Valley did nothing to offset the disaster war had brought to our lives), such songs as "If You're Going Back to Dixie" had moral worth. In the areas dealt with by the pages that follow, I see, looking back, that what my generation proposed to put in place of illusions had been formed by the illusions themselves. Then somewhere along its length the chain was broken. Do old people of every generation feel this? Probably; though present follies, intellectual follies not least, seem especially hopeless, persisted in despite all evidence.

I read some Freud before the war; was naturally aware of the opposition between Freudianism and Marxism, particularly the criticism from the left that psychoanalysis was too narrowly founded on the neuroses of the comfortably off. A few sought to reconcile the two philosophies or movements: in my slight and uninformed (and almost entirely non-public) way I would have classed myself among them. After the war I read much more in Freud and his followers, many of the ideas seeming truthful and appealing, not merely in matters concerning the psyche, and in art. The bold adumbrations in Freud's *The Future of an Illusion*, for instance, that every individual is virtually an enemy of civilization, and that the masses are lazy and unintelligent, came to seem closer to reality than the belief in proletarian virtue held before the war. Quite soon my verse began to express the strange intellectual ambivalence of our times: on the one hand, that though bourgeois society has great qualities it is doomed for not working well; and that though its replacement by a juster and more efficient order is theoretically plausible, what seems likely to occur in fact is a way of life finally repressive for all save dim or congenital yea-sayers. There are other obvious contradictions: the "Dixie complex" (subsuming in that phrase other copybook-heading qualities, like hard, selfless work; sacrifices for the next generation; and so forth) persists in the Soviet Union — despite hypocrisies — as it has drooped here since, say, the 1880s. Hence the continuing appeal of quite orthodox Marxism to idealistic youth, "exposures" of the communist world notwithstanding.

The narration of my life in *Souvenirs* ended before my own idealistic youth was over. The book itself came out in 1980, a few days after my sixty-eighth birthday. A hearteningly sympathetic review of it in *The Sunday Times* by John Carey prompted a letter from someone I had known as a young shorthand-typist with T. and F. Wylie Kay, the firm of Blackpool solicitors I was articled to in 1928. Though living in the country, she was staying with her daughter in London and suggested a meeting.

When that occurred, what Muriel had to say, necessarily compressing the time-scale and turns of fortune, would have beggared a novelist's imagination and skill, though she herself (born a little earlier than I) embodied quite recognizably the personable girl familiar more than fifty years before. She had had more than her fair share of ups and downs: a marriage with a cousin, not successful; the happiness and prosperity of a second go fairly soon interrupted by the husband's illness and in consequence a restricted way of life; death of the second husband, and of a third — this outline not exhausting the Balzacian or Bennettesque elements in her narration — an *Old Wives' Tale* indeed.

The few words she said of myself as I appeared in my far-off articled clerk days, though uncritically uttered, revealed me as a prig, and a somewhat devious one at that. In the typists' room, it seemed I used to inveigh against the use of the word "nice" and tell them to read D. H. Lawrence and Rabelais. From this distance of time, the literary advice seems more designed to soften the girls up with the erotic and scatological than to free their instinctive natures. A dotty Lawrentianism had superimposed itself on my socialistic beliefs after I had left school at sixteen, and it was a little time before the socialism showed through again, and in sharper form. I remember spending a fair part of the working day gassing in the typists' room, though perhaps only when the racing bets had been discussed and placed or the members of the bridge four in the articled clerks' room not all available. Occasionally one would be discovered among the typists by one of the managing clerks, whose touch of exasperation or irascibility was not too hard to bear. Less frequently, the junior partner, F. Wylie Kay (to whom I was articled), would catch me idling there, wasting the typists' time, and, as in my schooldays when surprised by the Boss, I would maladroitly feign some legitimate conversation or activity.

An irony not lost on me was that the meeting with Muriel took place at my suggestion in the Ladies' Annexe of the Athenaeum, conveniently half way between her daughter's flat and my own house. Quite apart from indicating the distance travelled from the codpieces and dark loins previously recommended, the venue may have encouraged her to think the development of my life had C. P. Snovian undertones, though even my membership of this club was unsought. It would be hard to detect a novelistic intelligence, however far from first-rate, behind the paths of my destiny. For instance, the cliché of early leftism yielding to elderly rightism — let alone a god-that-failed syndrome — would be essentially wide of the mark. I see a fundamental respect for authority even in my preference for Stalin over Trotsky in the Thirties; yet I suppose most who have known me in various professional activities would scarcely class me as conformist.

When I told Muriel that Lees (the former engrossing clerk at Wylie Kay's, described at some length in *Souvenirs*) was the only link I now had with that Blackpool existence of old, she said that he had scorned her because she had been educated at Elmslie, the poshest girls' private school in the town. Though Lees for his own amusement may well have heightened the drama of this attitude, I could well understand it, for he tended to despise anything not chosen or gained under one's own steam; nor would he have allowed virtue in a complete transformation of native speech or habits effected by education or money. One aspect of his admiration for Arnold Bennett was the latter's retention in the world of yachts (and Pall Mall clubs) native provincial instincts and scepticism. Muriel also said that the girl Lees so discreetly courted and came to marry had been her successor at Wylie Kay's — indeed that her father was responsible for getting the girl the job. Muriel's father had been friendly with F. Wylie Kay (hence Muriel's own appearance in the typists' room); was in fact the general manager of the large local co-operative society. He had suggested to FWK that Muriel's replacement should be the young daughter of his butchery department's manager, just qualified as a shorthand-typist, to wit the future Mrs Lees.

I relate this for the assumed curiosity of the readers of *Souvenirs*, also to emphasise the coincidental and implausible elements in ordinary life. Those can be accounted for by the closeness of society and the congruent interests of its members, mystery caused by links being forgotten in retrospect; though I think the novelist Anthony Powell might see in the business some aspect of the occult. Naturally, amatory affairs provide extreme examples, since they depend so much on easy opportunity: those of my Blackpool contemporaries when I was a young man taking on the set-to-partners convolutions of an Iris Murdoch novel. I do not know whether I shall in decency be able to indicate any of the permutations and combinations, so the reader may imagine them taking place almost at random.

Further as to re-writing autobiography, I may have been wrong in *Souvenirs* to have spared the reader more details of my early arrival at socialistic beliefs. The conversion of the hero of my novel *The Ruined Boys* echoes my own, but it was in the "boarders' library" not on a second-hand book barrow, that I found Robert Blatchford's *Merrie England*; my reading of the *Fabian Essays in Socialism* taking place later, when I had become pretty familiar with the ideas of Wells and Shaw through their imaginative works. Even at that tender age — possibly fourteen; surely barely fifteen — I was ready for Blatchford's simple and seemingly incontrovertible arguments and statistics about the material inequalities (and hence the injustices) in the capitalist system, viz English society. Strangely enough, I do not recall being moved one way or the other by the General Strike of 1926. It was memorable merely through the usual transport not being available to take the boarders to the playing fields, and my having to help carry one of the cricket bags the several miles involved. The bag may well have contained the Hobbs and oil-heavy bats soon to be described, which would have made it a burden indeed. And I seem to recall that the boy who held the other handle was Hamlet, later of the leper-colony. Possibly only one such foot-passage was involved, for a hired charabanc comes into the saga at some juncture. Perhaps it was later that year, my fourteenth (following the oppression of the strike's aftermath), that my incident on the road to Damascus occurred — though how I learnt about what went on in the world of politics is obscure, since a newspaper at school was a rarity.

The omission in *Souvenirs* of some account of the conversion, and of the reading and thought that went on supporting it, was misleading if it suggested perfunctoriness in that region. For many years I continued to believe that the abolition of private production would release wealth and ideals sufficient to raise humanity, its day to day life, its art, to heights hitherto unattained; and reveal the brotherhood of the species behind the foolish masks of armies, flags and religions. However, the action I took was feeble enough, even allowing for my age and circumstances.

My mother, like her father, was a dyed-in-the-wool Tory. Undoubtedly my native secrecy, as well as the ineffectualness of the advancement of my beliefs, prevented undue alarm on her part in early days, though I do not expect she cared for what she heard when I talked about ideological matters. It may be, too, that she knew more and worried more, though saying little. Strange how ideas penetrate into the seemingly most ideas-proof family, lying about like bacteria, waiting for any reasonable medium on which to flourish. When at school I saw Busoni's face on a piece of sheet music belonging to Mr Tregenza, the master whose playing of classical music helped to open my ears, I had no notion that even before the First World War he had turned himself into a "modern" composer, perhaps did not think of him as a composer at all. Nor did my own first dim attempts at literary creation take account of modernism (unless such as Maeterlinck could be included in the term). Indeed, by the time I came to write anything decent some were beginning to think modernism passé, a view that has spread — and grew more and more congenial to me, as did the idea that Busoni would have done better to remain a composer who used "old-fashioned" harmonies (as would Szymanowski). In other words, one lived long enough to see disproved many propositions that seemed self-evident; the relegation of many figures thought for ever vital; theories of history made irrelevant by the attenuation of the time required to prove them.

The atrocious Spengler once wrote (in a work translated into

English as *The Hour of Decision*) that the long "peace period from 1870 to 1914, and the memory of it, rendered all white men self-satisfied, covetous, void of understanding, and incapable of bearing misfortune." As to that period, being born in 1912 I scarcely lived in it and certainly do not recall it (unless I was under two and a half when lifted up by a neighbour to inhale, as a specific for whooping-cough, the fumes from a road-menders' great, high vessel for boiling tar). But my character surely came out of the softness of the epoch, if not marked by every single one of Spengler's derogatory epithets.

In the same work Spengler speaks of the spiritual weakness of "the 'Late' man of the higher civilizations, who lives in his cities cut off from the peasant and the soil and thereby from the *natural* experiencing of destiny, time, and death": this spiritual weakness is the "dread of reality." I will not further reproduce Spengler's Nietzschean acceptance — welcoming — of the consequences of man being "a beast of prey" and of history's frightful inevitabilities, except to transcribe the following from the book's introduction, written in Munich in July 1933:

> Greatness and happiness are incompatible and we are given no choice. No one living in any part of the world of today will be happy, but many will be able to control by the exercise of their own will the greatness or insignificance of their life-course. As for those who seek comfort merely, they do not deserve to exist.

There tends to be a Spenglerian movement in the individual life, as in collective history. In many old ages the dread of reality increases or at any rate is more frankly recognized; simultaneously, a sense of guilt may mature at having opposed (or, more accurately, passively resisted) the era, instead of ruthlessly making the most of what it offered. At the time Spengler was writing the words quoted, I would have been well aware of my cowardice, my flinching from unpleasantness, my general wish for things to be cosy — yet the drive and vigour of youth gave a certain power to the desire for one's ideals to prevail. Despite the example of the admired poets of 1916–18, I was far from the pacifism also anatomized and derided by Spengler, anticipating a good deal of trouble before men could be both great and happy. Foreseen, for one thing, was a struggle on the lines of the October Revolution, in which one would be "shitting with fear but confident of life."

The line comes from a poem of mine, probably contemporaneous with Spengler's words, that envisaged the armed struggle for socialism; a poem fortunately failing to achieve publication. The embarrassing phrase indicates both a general and personal need to conquer cowardice so as to bring a just society. My life, a cut-off, urban life, so scathingly identified by Spengler, had not fitted me for courage. As related in *Souvenirs*, there had been domestic pain and the rigours of a curious boarding-school, but these had merely magnified my longing for happy endings — a longing which, allied with compassion, helped to motivate my socialistic beliefs.

In a sense so modest as to be ironic, it turned out that I was among "the many", in Spengler's adumbration, able to control the status of my "life-course". Greatness may have always been beyond me, but of my own volition I gave up politics and, later, an active military role — and, on the other side of my life, never carried through the kind of fictional writing that might have brought wider recognition. As to the last, after *Image of a Society* had been quite successfully brought out in 1956, Leonard Russell, then literary editor of the *Sunday Times* and a devotee of an earlier novel, *The Second Curtain*, thoughtfully invited my wife and me to dine, the other guests being Mr and Mrs J. B. Priestley, and the generous object of the exercise to advance my fictive career. Priestley had read *Image of a Society*, was kind about it, but said he had wanted it longer, to tell him things about the characters he felt baulked at not knowing, and so forth. In a way I agreed with him, for I knew only too well I was a constipated writer, and probably only half-heartedly defended the book, if at all. But of course the truth of the matter was that I could only have extended it in a manner that would not have really wooed the public. My novels were then perhaps, certainly eventually became, if not *avant garde* in the sense that term is usually employed about fiction, at any rate pretty far from the "good read" a public expects. What I did come away from the Russells' unreservedly envying was Priestley's brilliant power, through mimicry and recall of detail, to evoke the music hall and "varieties" of the past, his epoch being just before the one I myself remember with affection but with miserably little talent to evoke.

Though the coming of the Second World War accorded with Spenglerian philosophy and prediction, it was followed (had he lived to see it Spengler would have been as surprised by it as I) by a "peace period" for "White men" which has lasted, as I write in the summer of 1980, nearly as long as the one he referred to. There

8

has been time even for those who apparently chose insignificance to have acquired a status somewhat above it. During these thirty-five years I re-read Spengler's *Decline of the West*, or parts of it, particularly the masterly Introduction. Its fatalism and pessimism fitted my post-war verse; the Spenglerian answer to history's dirty work (in nasty times be yourself nasty) being omitted by me. Yet the poetry always contained an escape clause: a lingering belief in the eventual triumph of human good, such as in the late Twenties and early Thirties I thought quite simply would be brought about by the establishment of world socialism. Also, the long survival ensured that the bonuses of human existence — the observation of nature, for example — became more and more precious, and so gave mere living a value and purpose outside the ideological considerations youth thought essential.

Greatness or insignificance, doom or utopia, fascism or communism — such alternatives proved to be less absolute than I'd imagined. Moreover, being possessed simultaneously by a belief in, and despair about, humanity, seemed in the end a fairly fruitful way of regarding the times through the medium of verse. The habit of mind of youth, my youth, to see the world as an arena of either/or, to seek single reasons, to find dogma and invent one's own — that has not entirely left me, particularly in the sphere of art, though even there I seem to have relented somewhat in recent years. Dylan Thomas, abstract art, "modern dance", Stockhausen (for instance) — all N.B.G. Yes, but Dylan Thomas wrote two or three sensible poems, and prose that one has to admit is occasionally quite funny; and abstraction has allowed some painters to hide in a decorative way their inadequate technique and poor eye for reality.

But mightn't I have been happier as a crank? Though one assents to the proposition that man is a beast of prey, one recognizes in oneself and some others the markings of what I once called in a quatrain "a species absurd" — a non-predatory human, still displaying aggression on occasions but always ready to roll on his back or fly off; non-grudge-bearing, also. Some ever-present sense of the practicable stopped me short of pacifism or vegetarianism, though in the final analysis it might have to be admitted that the impossibility of the entire human race adopting such creeds must mean its inevitable doom.

Not long after writing the foregoing about Spengler, I read in an excellent lecture by J. P. Stern, printed in the *T.L.S.*, October 10, 1980, that the summer of 1911 was the time of the Moroccan crisis "which ended with a profound humiliation of Wilhelm II's colonial aspirations and in which Spengler ... saw the seed of a major European conflict." Professor Stern also says, apropos of *The Decline of the West*, that its "catchy title and main ideas and structure ... were conceived" (as I was myself) in that same summer, one of unusual heat (as mentioned in *Souvenirs*). How fascinating and depressing to come across, in this lecture, Spengler's ideas once again, so right and yet so wrong! No wonder, after youthful certainties, that one moved into ambiguities, and stayed there. Professor Stern emphasises how Spengler "aestheticized" history (that makes him especially appealing to poets), and brings out splendidly the insights and illogicalities of Spengler's position. "Mankind," Spengler says, "is either a mere zoological term or a meaningless abstraction." How often one has felt this during the repeated follies of one's era!

And yet one has never quite ceased to believe in the possibility of the victory of human good. The contradiction is rather like Spengler believing in Germany's future (I put the thing crudely) though deploring the path she was being led down, forgetting that the more frightful the path the more it accorded with his view of history.

2 Summers of the Past

*I can't imagine a century
being made by Spender.
Was Fuller ever more
than a good tail-ender?*

— Gavin Ewart: "The Cricket of my Friends"

My father died in 1920 when I was eight. Though he took me to
Boundary Park and Watersheddings, where the Oldham soccer and
Rugby League teams played, I do not recall ever watching cricket
with him. There would have been Lancashire League cricket in
Oldham; and Old Trafford would not have been too awkward of
access in his Overland motor car, later the Crossley — at any rate
before we moved at the end of the 1914–18 war to Waterhead, on
the side of Oldham farthest from Manchester. Being brought up in
Scotland, perhaps he was less attached to cricket than football. And
yet having written that, don't I associate those villages and small
towns not far from Waterhead — Delph, Upper Mill, Milnrow,
Crompton — not only with dark stone walls and mills but also
little cricket league-tables in the Oldham paper, and white figures
against the lush green of levels on the valley sides? And that was
a country we quickly left after my father's death.

I first played cricket myself when I went to boarding-school in
Blackpool in 1923, though I participated in a species of the game
at earlier times on Blackpool sands or, across the road from Happy
Valley, in the informally-named Sparrow Park, a patch of grass,
with benches, rockeries, and a mast like that of a large yacht. The
sand pitches could be hard, recently left by the tide; or soft,
untidewashed, clogging the feet as in a nightmare. I was never any

11

good at cricket, but in the end played for the school XI, a non-bowler going in at a bowler's number. rather like some of the county captains, obligatorily amateurs in those days.

I did not think I should write further about that time, least of all about cricket, but memories have risen whose interest to me I hope to communicate, despite having come across the following the other night in *The Life of Henri Brulard* (Stendhal's autobiography), much to the point and very off-putting: "who the deuce will have the courage to wade through it [i.e. his early memoirs], to read this excessive pile of *Is* and *Mes*? I even find it stinking myself. That's the weakness of this sort of writing in which, moreover, I cannot season the insipidity with any sauce of charlatanism." I remember several of the cricket bats we played with at school. One was known as "the Hobbs", a heavy implement bearing the master's signature in facsimile, which I tried to avoid in early days but disliked less as I grew taller and stronger. Another, smaller in size, was almost equally heavy because someone had once over-zealously left it in linseed oil overnight. What insipidity!

In one way I liked cricket; in another, not. In the playground at school during the summer term cricket of a kind was played by senior boys, to which I eventually graduated, initially insinuating myself at the edge of the "field", in fact the walls of the bogs. A solid rubber ball and the asphalt surface provided passable conditions. The oil-soaked bat was available for use, for I recall its toe leaving a mark on the asphalt when one pressed on it taking guard. Sometimes a master joined in the game, Mr David, who was good enough to play on occasions for Blackpool's Second XI. I enjoyed these sessions: late in my schooldays I began to see what cricket was about. Two elementary instances may be given. A boy called Burton used to attack the leg stump with good-length balls. He was below medium pace but not a spinner, extreme accuracy the secret of his success, though perhaps doing a little both ways. Eventually I realised one had to play forward to the pitch of the ball, bat close to the forward leg, if one wasn't to be bowled at an early stage (topography required that the stumps be chalked on a wall, and fielders positioned on the on side, except for a fellow who could lurk in the space in front of the classrooms' entrance, just too far to make an effective silly mid-off). A boy called Heys did bowl at medium pace, and his getting his head almost too well out of the way of his arm at the moment of delivery (faintly reminiscent of Alec Bedser, then aged about nine) demonstrated what for years I had only dimly perceived — that the arm should be vertical when the hand released the ball. Real cricketers will smile in their sleeves at such confessions.

I imitated the foregoing and other players, particularly Mr David's bowling action (which included in the run-up an exaggerated but catchy piston motion of the fist holding the ball), but never had a word of coaching. Without natural ability, therefore, improvement was meagre. I visualised clearly the actions my body ought to perform but it was not well enough co-ordinated to perform them. I watched with amazement a younger and quite ordinary boy called Bancroft dance down the wicket to drive. What unjust deity had conferred such professional ability? In all this I see a parallel to my first attempts to write: imitation, snail-like improvement, execrable performance.

The side of cricket I didn't like was to be found at the school's playing fields. Soon after I joined the school it lost its playing field to the speculative building of the day, just gathering pace, and moved out to what had been agricultural land at Squires Gate. The pitches followed the slope of the terrain, not inconsiderable. I remember well their location being chosen — stones removed, coarse grass cut, the big roller pulled by ropes; the boarders' labour being lavishly applied, like that of Israel in Egypt. A cricket table was a thing unknown, even for the "first game", so bowling of any accuracy was formidable, medium pace or over inclining to the lethal. Most, including myself, played in gym shoes; no guard at all against a rap by the ball on ankle or toe. In the lower games one pad or none was *de rigueur*, simply through shortages. Late in my school career I won a pair of batting-gloves in the school sports, perhaps had a season, or rump of a season, wearing them: presumably they slightly relieved my apprehension at standing up to a bowler of any pace. Even on the first pitch there were sometimes pick-up games. If I were choosing and won the toss for choice I was torn between picking Burton, the soundest, and the demon Foreshew, wanted so I would not have to face his speed, which his captain always took care to augment by letting him bowl down the slope aforesaid. It comes to me that at the last I was cricket secretary (no doubt chosen for literary ability, limited though that was in wider spheres), sending the ritual postcards to other school secretaries — "We can offer you 9th or 23rd June for the match here . . ." This would account for me sometimes choosing a pick-up side

(Captain's XI v. Secretary's XI), perhaps the principal reason why I got a place in the First XI.

The main school fixture to arrange was with Southport College, whose team included Caldwell, a bowler Mr David had pronounced the fastest schoolboy bowler he had ever seen; no mean bat, either. Did I face him twice? I recall only the home game, when I actually caught him in the deep, falling back into a gorse-bush (if boundaries were ever marked at Squires Gate they would any way incorporate extraneous vegetation), having previously dropped him from another towering whack. By the time I came in to bat he had turned to bowling enormous but extremely slow off-breaks from the bottom of the slope, the sort of undeserved luck I've been conscious of all my life. Plainly, Caldwell had become one of those prodigies whose talents are so ripe they decay a little even in youth. I had scored half a dozen when the ball slipped from his hand as he attempted a great tweak, and rolled gently towards me. I stood watching it fail to reach the batting crease, gravelled to know what to do, perhaps even joining in the derisory laughter. "Why didn't you go down the pitch and hit it hard with a golf shot?" Mr David asked afterwards. "You couldn't have been caught — the ball was on the ground." The lost opportunity nagged and nagged me, particularly as I was dismissed soon after, not by Caldwell.

Writing this, I see myself in the charabanc bound for the away fixture with Southport College, in some way indisposed, travelling as scorer, in fact. The neck area is in question, for was I not collarless, bandaged? I couldn't have been suffering from tonsillitis, even quinsies, as I did more than once in those days, for in that case I should have been in bed. The ailment must have been a boil, I guess: the coward's boil, not the liar's quinsy.

I was happier at an earlier age, solitarily (or comparing notes only with some serious friend, like Hamlet) playing paper cricket. I expect the procedure is still well-known. I assigned a symbol to each letter of the alphabet (e.g. 4, 2, lbw, caught), then opened a book at random and, following the letters on the page, played the match I had decided on. I used to alter the symbolism until reasonable verisimilitude was achieved: one couldn't have a county side, let alone England or Australia, dismissed for peanuts, half of them hit wicket. But having got a decent balance I did not stick to it, perhaps craving continual surprise, as in watching real cricket. I used to keep bowling analyses, but more elaborate refinements such as county tables and Test Match series were beyond my powers of application, like much else worthwhile in life. I don't think I ever descended, as did some, to mingling myself, or even school heroes like the great Wetton (whose humiliation will later be touched on), with real cricketers, but I would arrange a few matches out of my head, as it were; for instance, players with names starting with "H" v. the Rest. Hobbs, Holmes, Hallows, Hendren, Hirst, Hitch, Hearne — good grief, does my memory fail so early in the list?

Some time during my boyhood the Blackpool municipality established a park, Stanley Park, in an area then behind the town. Near the park's main entrance was the ground used by the Blackpool C.C. Whether it was there already or set up as part of the park's amenities I do not know. Though (like Squires Gate) always in my time a low-scoring pitch, it achieved county status, helped by the promise of spectators in decent numbers from summer visitors. Perhaps a county match a season was played there, plus a week of festival cricket at the "back end", viz September. To many of these matches I went as a boy, later as a solicitor's articled clerk.

I have not looked up Wisden or other works, so in what I shall say I am sure to get things wrong. But the record will have memory's peculiar purity. In the film *Bonnie and Clyde* there is a marvellous scene of family reunion before the inevitable permanent separation of the criminals from the innocent, which the director shot as though it were happening in a sea-mist. That sort of sad and legendary unclarity is not quite what I am aiming for: indeed, some memories are sharp, though resemble snapshots rather than film sequences.

Some members of the Lancashire team of the later Twenties come first to recall. Makepeace, who opened, was a notorious slowcoach, a stonewaller and a half. Do I rightly visualise him as under medium height, gnome-like, even bow-legged? The last-named characteristic would tie in with his playing soccer for Everton, many good footballers being thus configured. Certainly his appearance and character were from a typical mould of Lancastrian, the sort of chap I might sit opposite to in the Waterhead tram, and take in, a few years before. Except when Lancashire's fate was in the balance, I was always relieved to see him go — in those days, to a degree still, of the essentially frivolous mind that likes the *adagio* to end and the *scherzo* begin. His partner, Hallows, (what divine fictioneer chose these names?), could not avoid appearing dashing by contrast, but he was in any case admirable, and, as I thought then, should have played more representative cricket. Did Ernest

Tyldesley come in when Makepeace or Hallows was out, or was he at number four? Tyldesley (E) was a great batsman, no doubt without the final polish of Hobbs, the final sparkle of Hendren, but utterly reliable, yet fluent and aesthetically satisfying. I am not sure but that he, too, was of archetypal Lancastrian breed, though possibly merely as to wearing his cap like Makepeace, at no angle at all. I had a soft spot for Farrimond, a batsman-wicketkeeper usually kept from better things by Duckworth, England's and Lancashire's regular keeper. I suppose his name stimulated my liking, especially as against the common-sounding Duckworth: Farrimond — aristocratic syllables. But I must add, in the manner of Dr Johnson about his cat Hodge, Duckworth was a good wicketkeeper, too.

Tyldesley was usually pronounced in Blackpool "Tiddlesy". This is not the only example I shall provide of the town's deficiency in elocutionary prowess. Very nearly as famous as Ernest was Dick Tyldesley. In my day he was extremely stout, perhaps had always been so, giving the first impression that he was past his best, which was not the case. The impression was reinforced by his trousers being held up by a necktie, surely a habit from an earlier epoch. He was a slow right-arm bowler, bringing his arm from behind his waist (or, rather, where that once had been) in a fashion that initially seemed amateurish, a schoolboy's action. All he did was interesting, though flight of great daring was his hallmark. When he came in, low down in the order, his bat seemed fragile, wielded somewhere below his stomach, but he slogged effectively.

I saw — didn't I? — McDonald in Warwick Armstrong's Australian side before he played for Lancashire. Even in my nonage I realised he was a beautiful bowler, an adjective sometimes used loosely today — "Buggins bowled beautifully" meaning no more perhaps than kept the run-rate down. In McDonald's case it was strictly deserved. His run-up was long but compact, the slightly flapping black hair the untidiest part of the business. He was very much sideways on when his arm started to come over, and how it came over was the perpetual mystery, the chief constituent of the pulchritude. It must have been high like Heys's, yet at some point it seemed to bend, as though following the most economical orbit, a moment of suppleness and grace that nevertheless one felt was adding power to the delivery.

The action of Cecil Parkin, fast-medium, was at the opposite pole. His run-up was long-striding, spiderlike, both arms held away from the body. "Parkin", I might announce during playground cricket, and do a fair imitation of the action if not the result. I think he also bowled slower stuff, of an eccentric nature, like Caldwell's. On the field he provided pretty continuous comedy (or, at the least, diversion), probably a man of pessimism or secret sorrow. I verily believe he was the originator of that flip of the boot that brings a ball travelling on the ground conveniently up into the bowler's hand. The trick — then almost a novelty — was expected by the crowd, but he did not always satisfy expectations, feigning to miss the ball with his boot, or even not to see it. Similarly, he would occasionally pretend to misfield or, what was more effective, pretend *not* to have misfielded, throwing a merely imaginary ball to the wicketkeeper. He batted perhaps as low as number ten; always hit out extravagantly, and was quite capable of making runs. I once saw him given out lbw, and his being the tenth wicket down, the innings closed — the umpires removing the bails, everyone starting to walk off. Except Parkin, who with extreme naturalness affected not to have seen the umpire's finger go up, and took careful guard for the next ball. When he found himself alone at the wicket, he gave a start of surprise, and followed the players to the pavilion. The mime was rapid but explicit, absolutely not overdone.

When I went to Stanley Park as a schoolboy I expect my mother made me sandwiches for the luncheon interval. I would visit one of the refreshment tents for a ginger-beer, then to be had in stone bottles, very good. When I went as an articled clerk, probably with others from the office, we would buy from a tent pork pies and ginger-beer shandies, pints. The pies were also very good — oval, deep, fresh, crisp pastry, peppery. Inside the refreshment tents was gloom after the summer outdoors, the strange grass floor mostly trampled down, the walls sometimes flapping like McDonald's hair, abandoned score-cards littering the ground, a constant ebb and flow of male customers. "I had not thought death had undone so many," I might have quoted had I known the verse, then not long written.

Again early observed in connection with cricket was the incongruity of reality and history (or literature), a sense that came even more strongly from the few race-meetings I went to when an articled clerk. To experience the irrelevancies, accidents, banalities and tediums of actuality through the subjective vision, and then to see the rich and contradictory process in the newspaper the next day subsumed in the bare, brief lists of scores (e.g. "O'Connor lbw 43") made one speculate on the nature of experience. I carried into my early fictive efforts an obsession with the problems of naturalism and formality, so well exemplified by cricket and its records: the *Ulysses* complex, one might call it, after the novel that in my earliest cricketing days had, like *The Waste Land*, been only fairly recently completed.

In the festival cricket at Stanley Park when the season proper was over, I watched a good many players, some legendary, but mere enumeration would be superfluous. I didn't in the least mind that the matches were in essence as meaningless as those of my paper-cricket — Lancashire v. Mr A. E. R. Gilligan's XI, North v. South. One was sustained by the procession of characters, the perennial promise of extraordinary action, and, above all, the fleshing out of fable. One actually saw Root bowling his "leg theory" — short, low-trajectory balls on the leg side, a good few of which the batsmen ignored. Boring after a bit, but it must be remembered that curiosity about the great or notorious was then only to be satisfied at first-hand, newsreels (for years silent ones) and photographs merely tantalising. Good looks, the angle of a cap — such adventitious things often attracted my especial interest and allegiance, as in the case of O'Connor of Essex, before-mentioned, who at last did play for England, as I earnestly hoped he would. I remember an early appearance of Kenneth Farnes, also of Essex, then at Cambridge or (as will be seen) more likely about to go up, his exotic cap and amateur's initials giving a first impression of effeteness, quickly dissipated when he came on to bowl with super-Caldwellian speed. One got to know the Essex players, and those of Northants and Glamorgan, for Stanley Park was allowed to entertain only the less glamorous counties.

Farnes was killed in the war. One is tempted to think of 1939 as marking the end of the best epoch of one's absorption in cricket, but really the terminal date was earlier. For one thing, I never played after I left school in 1928. For another, in youth and adolescence cricket-watching, like many another activity, held promise of adventure on the side, not strictly connected with the game yet by no means making the experience of it impure.

Chronology has misted up, like that scene in *Bonnie and Cylde*. In 1938 I saw Bradman squatting in the outfield at Lords, plucking a blade of grass to chew, humming to himself. My thought was: I must remember this for posterity. But here I am at sixty-eight, Bradman still alive — reported in *The Times* this very morning as saying that Vivian Richards is the best on-side player he has ever seen. Was it before or after the war I saw a Lancashire League poster proclaiming (on separate lines) "Nelson with Constantine" versus some team or other — the "Nelson with" in tiny letters, the "Constantine" huge? Before the war, I believe — yet I almost overlapped with the great man on the BBC Board of Governors in the Seventies. Perhaps this is the place to say that despite my previous remark about checking, I did look in the London Library to confirm the death of Farnes, feeling that memory alone ought not to kill off one so young and so endowed — and accidentally found his book, *Tours and Tests*, published in 1940. It is a work still readable, containing some interesting opinions and observations, and of a Stendhalian self-deprecation. Typical of its modesty is the frontispiece photograph bearing the legend "H.M. King George V examining Wyatt's thumb." Farnes himself is in the background, recognizable by his great height. To my chagrin I found his description of McDonald far better than mine. Strangely enough, it occurs in his account of a match Essex played against Lancashire in 1930, at Blackpool (one of several county matches he appeared in before his university days). Undoubtedly I was there. Here is the passage:

> He was then about thirty-eight years old, yet he was still fast, and still preserved that beautiful action — the most nearly perfect possible. He took quite a long run, working up easily to a maximum speed at the moment of delivery. As he reached the crease his left arm straightened sharply and pointed straight above him. The whole thing with the follow-through was extremely graceful and rhythmic, a "grooved" action, seemingly effortless. Yet the ball became a thing of vivid life as it left his hand. McDonald, Duckworth has told me, had very long arms and amazingly supple shoulders; he could put both arms over his head and clasp his hands under his chin. He could use the full width of the crease, and so was able to avoid any holes caused by the bowling which inconvenience most bowlers. And in spite of his speed, he was so light that he could have bowled in dancing pumps.

That my novel, *The Ruined Boys* (1959), included a school cricket match indicates continuing interest. The scene, passionate but farcical, like much in sport, is invented, though the idea of the player Wilkes came from Caldwell. I altered his description in the general pursuit of avoiding defamation. There is a bit of business about the scoring, which I would regard as generally interesting, in the same, fundamentally odd, way as my chance-produced paper cricket figures used to interest me. Only the numeration relevant to the nub of the game is given, for my novels usually stick to the matter in hand, but had I been more indulgent I would have assumed a willingness on the reader's part to be told, for instance, Wilkes's bowling analysis for the season to date.

As well as physical and mathematical beauty, sentiment comes into the sport, of course. During the First World War, the musicologist Edward J. Dent said that "people like George Robey make me feel patriotic". One knows precisely what he meant — and it could be said of rather more cricketers than comedians. E. V. Lucas (I read in *The Lyttelton — Hart-Davis Letters*) "was chary of seeing the greatest of all jugglers, Cinquevalli, because he always made him cry". I once saw Hendren take a low catch close-in from a fierce hit, all so quickly done the ball seemed for a few moments to vanish; and simultaneously there came to mind a previously read opinion that Hendren was the greatest short-leg in the world. Didn't there brim a Cinquevallian tear?

3 Vamp Till Ready

At night a city narrows into a populous café.
At night the city of the dead becomes a shrunken framework.
Into which pour mincingly those uninspired wanderers.

— Laura Riding

Gilbert Waller joined Seafolde House as a dayboy at the same time as I went there as a boarder. Similarly to my own case, the Headmaster had underestimated his abilities, and after a term he moved up with me, skipping a form. When I think of him at this moment I am reminded of the start of *Madame Bovary*, though his character was far from that of Charles Bovary. But first encountering him then was, as with Bovary in Flaubert's novel, a memorable though oblique way into an entire story, in which, however, he came to play only a subsidiary and eventually off-stage part.

The chiming of his surname with my own struck me, at the age of eleven, as of significance in some mystico-coincidental way: his long head, and face narrow rather than otherwise, were also common possessions. But there was no deep physical resemblance: Waller presented an owlish aspect, the immobile-save-for-blinking characteristic being exaggerated in the face of authority, or in stubborn or impudent mood. When, a little later, I visited his home in holiday time, his mother said to him, perhaps more than once: "Why can't you stand up straight, like Roy?" So I suppose the owlishness was accompanied by something of a stoop, though he could never be classed as really tall.

His interests were unscientific, in fact proved in a way to be literary. But rather in the manner of Hamlet's injecting his spots with Euthymol, he once demonstrated, by swallowing and effortlessly regurgitating a largish fragment of apple, that the stomach

21

(or, rather, the oesophagus) would reject anything not digestible. I was sufficiently impressed to have remembered the experiment for nearly sixty years, but was not convinced the theory was a sound one. There was something prestigious in the business, plausible at first blush but not withstanding reflection — journalistic, one might say. And a journalist was what Waller became.

For the foot in the door, picture-snatching side of the journalist's craft, Waller was plainly fitted from an early age. It must have been at the Boarders' Concert of our first year that he stood on a desk seat and sang "The Lass with a Delicate Air". Day-boys were encouraged to attend this evening function, though I do not recall any other instance of them otherwise participating, or, indeed, of any other impromptu or unsolicited contribution, which Waller's certainly was. His services were offered (probably to Mr David, the master always in charge of the affair) and the song begun, in determined fashion. The unhasty climbing on the desk-seat so as to be properly seen and heard was a Wallerish touch added after the extra item had been allowed.

The performance was impressive if one cared for that sort of thing: a strong, tuneful treble issuing from the full lips, inclined to be pursed even when not in song — the gaze steady through the round spectacles, challenging ridicule, though promising complete indifference should catcalls come. My head full of Tosti and Amy Woodforde-Finden, Michael Arne's tune seemed recherché, even highbrow. Waller may well have learnt it not at his previous school but at home, where elements of an intellectual life-style existed. His father was a commercial artist: his connections with the local newspaper probably helped Waller in due time to secure work on it as a cub reporter. His mother was a pretty woman, domestically capable; her moral fibre indicated by her approval of an upright stance. Allinson's flour (whole meal implied) is particularly specified in the parkin recipe she supplied to my mother (who copied it into her recipe book), so there may have been health-food undertones in the Waller household:

¾lb Allinson's flour. ¼lb fine oatmeal. 6ozs butter. 4ozs sugar. 1 egg. 3 large tablesps syrup, 1 of black treacle. 1 teasp each of cinnamon, salt, bi-carb. 2 teasp ginger. Little milk to mix. Bake 1½ to 2 hours (presumably on about Mark 2).

Waller did not stay long at Seafolde House; was sent to be a boarder at some grammar school, I think with Quaker associations. Perhaps his parents had become rather more affluent, or had foreseen Seafolde House's decline, not an impossible piece of prognostication. My brother claims to know a precipitating reason. The senior boy called Wetton, previously mentioned, punched Waller. Later, Waller's father came into the school playground and asked a boy to point Wetton out, which the boy was able to do, Wetton being a famous character, centre-half in the school XI, a good off-spin bowler, a sharp dresser, and with sleeked-back yellow hair. Mr Waller then went over and punched Wetton, presumably with some words of explanation. The story need not be doubted, for Wetton was no stranger to violence, and Waller would certainly attract it.

During the rest of our mutual schooldays Waller and I were only tenuously in touch, yet when, after two years or so as a solicitor's articled clerk, I went to London for a couple of months at a law crammer's to prepare for the Law Society's Intermediate Examination, I met up with Waller once more. His parents may well have recommended the digs in Guilford Street to which I went, for Waller was then, or had recently been, living in them — more likely the latter because of the feud to be mentioned later; also I do not remember being in the place with him. However, recall of the time is utterly patchy. As in the Blackpool boarding-houses lived in during boyhood, I must have encountered noteworthy characters in Guilford Street, but all have faded. My brother says I told him of a fellow-lodger who at the time impressed himself on me. "There, can't you hear it?" he said to me. "What?" "The pigs' wireless." Enquiries as to my reception of this service took place on a few occasions, presumably over breakfast, the only communal activity; my answers always disappointing.

Waller's career as a provincial reporter had been interrupted to take a year's course in journalism at London University. Perhaps the first instance, in London at any rate, of his prevailing on me to do something foreign to my nature was his illegal invitation, knowing of my interest in the subject, to attend a lecture or seminar, part of the English Literature strand of his course, at University College. He had a proprietorial pride in the quality of these lectures; assured me I should without question be taken for a member of the course. The lecturer was J. Isaacs, later, if not then, a well-known academic. Discussion was encouraged after Isaacs's remarks: typical of my character that having gone into the lecture-room with apprehension

I should then argue, in the testy manner I already evinced on such collective occasions, with the lecturer. Our point of difference was my maintaining, against his dictum, that any worthwhile literary criticism was bound to be a matter of personal judgement not the application of formal principles. Needless to say, I did not appreciate the nuances of this controversy (which still goes on!); my stance being based on commonsense and the conviction, derived from D.H. Lawrence, of the primacy of gut feeling. Waller sat next to me with the smug satisfaction of one who, carrying a swordstick, sees an alsatian dog making a leap for him; an image less outré than might at first appear. Also, he had the true journalist's delight in rows, however mild or minor, coupled with the power sometimes to foment them.

His Diploma in Journalism, or whatever it was, acquired, he never returned to the *West Lancashire Evening Gazette*, but got a job, perhaps the editor's, on a rag called *The Holborn Gazette*, and later lived perilously on linage (that is, being paid, per line, only for stories actually printed) for the *Daily Express*. With merely a touch or two the boy soprano had transformed himself into a somewhat transatlantic idea of a journalist: a trenchcoat almost invariably worn; either no hat or a trilby with a brim turned down all the way round; cigarette in a holder; a hint of sideburns. It must be added that in the end he did become a regular reporter on the *Express*, and in its palmiest days. He would not necessarily have awaited that status before behaving in the manner appropriate to it. He may well have still been merely on linage when he took me over to sit down to drink with the great foreign correspondent Sefton Delmer in the Fleet Street Henekey's. And in due time even the transatlantic manner was justified.

During my London sojourns as an articled clerk I saw a good deal of Waller. In retrospect, that seems strange. Intellectually we had little in common, but he did introduce me to the records of such as Duke Ellington, Louis Armstrong, Joe Venuti, some of which (mainly the more *cantabile*, less frenetic parts) I liked a great deal. I think it wouldn't be unfair to say that his cultural grasp was journalistic — referring to Hemingway or Epstein, say, with plausible knowledgeableness. His way of life (though, as will be seen, the normality of his origins asserted itself in the end) had successive peaks of the bizarre, though the troughs of his existence were outlandish enough. In one of his bad economic spells, for instance — hanging on to Fleet Street, to a life in London at all, by his

24

eyebrows — his main meal at the café in Marchmont Street we used a lot was almost invariably tea and an "individual" syrup sponge, a far cry from his mother's cuisine.

Probably it would be early evening. He would enter the café, trenchcoat open, the *Evening Standard* in hand (probably a walking-stick as well), push his spectacles up with a forefinger, say to the man behind the counter: "Cupper tea and a golden pudding, Charley." The pronunciation thus of "cup of" seemed to acknowledge a life-giving or life-enhancing quality in the article referred to, something universal yet specially therapeutic — rather like the *Daily Express* of those days (the *Standard* was much more highbrow), which had a common enough touch to attract an enormous readership though its style was arguably a mere front for something almost sophisticated and cynical. A few of its contributors seemed self-consciously pastoral, like the cartoonist Strube with his character of the "Little Man", perhaps anticipating (though less odious than) Chaplin's use of the term "the Little Fellow" in the commentaries added to the reissue of his silent films.

Charley, the proprietor of the café was Spanish; provided good food at amazingly modest prices. The golden pudding was one of a number of concessions made in those pre-mass-foreign-travel days to an English cuisine. The cheapness of the delicacy (probably 3d, not more) and its satisfying quality were sufficient reasons for Waller's choice, yet allied to the tea it reflected or symbolized something in his being, fundamental yet hard to put a name to.

But Waller often expressed himself in more spectacular ways. Once he bought sneezing-powder from the joke-shop in New Oxford Street. The strategy for its use was that he and I should go separately into pubs and disseminate it to the discomfort of the drinkers — separately, so as to be less likely to fall under suspicion. Before our entries, the powder was sprinkled into the middle pages of Waller's *Evening Standard* and the newspaper then folded. At the bar, a half-pint ordered (usually mild, sometimes in public bars as cheap as 2½d), one or other of us would open the paper and, after a mock perusal of, say, Arnold Bennett's weekly books article, feign a sneeze, thus wafting the powder towards the nearby bar-flies.

The wheeze (the vocabulary of *The Magnet* or *The Gem*, magazines of our Seafolde House schooldays, comes appropriately to mind) actually worked, though a few hard looks were bent in our direction, perhaps our youth a tell-tale sign in those quiet pubs down the Gray's Inn Road which at that early time of evening were

25

patronized only by a few lingering craftsmen and the elderly proletarians of the quarter. Leaving, after a staggered interval to put the sneezers off the scent, as it were, as well as to enable us to savour the jest, Waller would positively chortle on the way to the next pub. "Did you see his pipe actually fall out of his mouth?" I recall him saying, apropos one victim assailed by an unanticipated sternutation.

I recounted in *Souvenirs* removing my collar and tie, and collecting for him near the Angel while he sang in the street. One of my trilby hats (perhaps the black bought for its imagined literary connotation) was used for the surprising number of coins collected in a short time. I believe this was a mere jape, like the sneezing-powder expeditions, unoccasioned by Waller's poverty, for the money was spent not on golden puddings but in a pub back in the purlieus of Bloomsbury. I was not altogether easy about standing in the gutter, holding out a trilby, black or otherwise, though at that epoch street entertainment by the needy was a commonplace. But I was embarrassed more by Waller's singing. The voice was as true and confident as in "The Lass with a Delicate Air" years before. The song featured at this later date was "Caller Herrin'". Typically, Waller knew all the words of Lady Nairne's lyric, not merely the opening invitation to purchase the fish in question. Though I don't think a Scottish accent was attempted, there was something irritating about the rendition, exacerbated by Waller's without hesitation finding a song so apt for a busker in that part of the metropolis (weren't we near the Sadler's Wells Theatre?) — well-known, but with an ambience acceptable to the educated, and a hint of starving mariners' families, if not of the brave fishermen themselves, actually present.

A final example of Waller's mania may be given. He had left the digs I was in, at enmity with the landlady and her spinster daughter. There is no reason to suppose he felt robbed or oppressed: more likely some louche behaviour of his promoted the antagonism. In any case, he had found a softer bed with a younger landlady, a grass widow, a few doors away. His entrée to his former digs possible through my own occupation, he conceived a campaign of revenge for real or imagined slights. On the penultimate day of my two-months' stay he hid a kipper behind one of the pictures in the dining-room; concealed, too, a depilatory substance called "Veet" which he claimed had also an objectionable smell. It was characteristic of his journalistic style, closely adapted to the requirements of the *Daily Express* of the time (perhaps perennially demanded of the popular journalist), that, as he told me, he later called at the digs on some pretext, maybe actually penetrating to the dining-room — at any rate claiming to have experienced the miasma in the house resulting from his concealments, and reflected in what he alleged were the haggard, haunted looks of the landlady. Those able to hear the pigs' wireless may have believed that broadcasting authority responsible. I should say, speaking of mania, that the walking-stick carried by Waller was a sword-stick, bought from the famous walking-stick and umbrella shop near the joke-shop he patronized, and with which, he said as confidently as he sang, he had once stabbed to the heart an alsatian dog that had injudiciously sprung at him.

His confession to canine homicide was made almost certainly soon after we re-met: it bears the hallmark of a lingering schooldays relationship, for at school tall stories are put out as gospel from some deep need of the young to boast and impress (need carried by many of us into old age). When I myself was asked if my father had worn a kilt during his Scottish upbringing, I said yes — qualifying what immediately seemed a too whopping affirmative by adding that of course it was a mere strip of cloth wrapped round the lower torso. I expect I jibbed at endowing my father with the elaborate sporran and so forth I had seen on the comedian Harry Lauder (a Lowlander, anyway), harking back for sartorial plausibility to the days of Culloden or Glencoe.

It would seem Waller had become a regular *Express* reporter by the time of my second London stay, for I accompanied him on two jaunts which would scarcely have been assigned to one merely on linage. The first was an attempt to interview Winston Churchill's daughter, Sarah, in the news because of her matrimonial affairs. She opened the door of her flat — we glimpsed Titian hair, a transparent complexion, a fine ankle — and smiled a couple of virtual "no comments", and closed it. When the story appeared I was astonished at Waller's resource in putting his own questions into the interviewee's mouth, as well as her own negatives, so enabling a few inches to be devoted to what had been an utter non-event.

On the other outing, Waller proposed to photograph a corpse, or, rather, have a corpse photographed by an *Express* photographer. The plot had been hatched before the evening in question. A young man had died in circumstances rumoured to be suspicious; perhaps poisoned by someone who wanted him out of the way. Even in those

27

days, when some popular newspapers could assume a readership rather than a viewership, there was a premium on pictures, but one of the deceased did not seem to exist. Had Waller read in American journalistic annals — perhaps on his London University course — of the cadaver-photo ploy? It may well have been so. The mortuary-keeper, or the relevant assistant (nominally a Shakespearean character, but his personality has not come down), had been squared (the amount of the bribe a mere two or three pounds), and we were admitted, out of office hours, so to speak, to institutional premises somewhere in North London. We had waited in a nearby pub till the time of assignation, and I at least had taken care to have a few whiskies to insulate me from any grisliness to come, rather like swallowing a seasickness remedy in a high wind at the quayside.

The nude corpse was wheeled out of refrigeration on a trolley, appropriately covered at first by the striped material of a butcher's apron. Emaciation emphasised the bony arch from which the pathetic genitals depended; red lines, like those indicating cuts of meat in a cookery book, showed the autopsy had already taken place. The eylids were drooping but sufficiently open: Waller attempted to comb the tangled hair but it started to come out in the comb's teeth. My task was to prop up the head to enable the photograph to be taken. My brother remembers that I told him I used a hammer for the purpose. Slightly mysterious how it came to be available, but the idea that I would be too fearsome to touch the body must be right since even now I prefer to interpose a spade between my hands and a dead bird. The photograph was duly printed, I think with some faking of a collar and tie; not too bizarre to those who had no reason to imagine it as otherwise from life. Almost simultaneously, the inquest, or adjourned inquest, discovered the death had been due to natural causes, so the story also died.

For occasions such as these Waller introduced me, when necessary, as from "the AP", which he said was the American equivalent of the PA, the initials providing credentials difficult immediately to verify. Similarly on a later occasion, when showing us over the *Express*, he introduced my future wife as "the sob-sister" on the *West Lancashire Evening Gazette*, though in fact she was the editor's secretary. Thus was one drawn at a stroke into Waller's world of instant and enduring fancy.

In the early days Waller's great friend in London was Alec

Marston. It may well have been Marston who put him on to such discs as Armstrong's "I'm a ding dong Daddy" and Ellington's "Hot and Bothered", a far cry from "The Lass with a delicate air". Marston played jazz piano and, I think, attempted the clarinet, though I am maybe confusing that instrument with the black, silver-knobbed walking-stick he usually carried at this epoch. Marston was tallish, pale, hair brushed straight back; quite a look of the comedian Sid Field — eyes even at that early age slightly poached. The walking -stick was a typical strand in his faintly seedy elegance, more than a touch of the Dick Swivellers — another being a black evening bowtie converted to day wear. He worked in an advertising agency: I think really was a copy-writer though hardly out of his teens, if that. Jazz was an amateur pursuit, but after the war he wrote some numbers for revues presented in a more or less low dive in Irvine Street.

I knew Marston already. The coincidence was not so great as might appear, for he was from Blackpool; must have come to be friendly with Waller through that connection, rather like the protagonists of "If You're Going Back to Dixie". My own knowledge of Marston arose in an even earlier epoch, at our kindergarden, in fact, Northlands High School, where he had stood out as a knowing and articulate infant, plump in the school's male uniform of white jersey, black-and-white horizontally-striped tie. After kindergarten our ways had parted, though my wife-to-be had known him in his later schooldays, also noting his confidence in worldly matters. Now the plumpness had vanished: the *savoir faire* and gift of the gab remained.

I fancy Marston, though his life-style was far from conventional, was less positively eccentric than Waller. He would have taken sneezing-powder and concealed kippers as everyday matters, if not going so far as to deal in them himself. It may have been Marston rather than Waller who introduced me to a set of characters hanging about Soho cafés, particularly the Café Bleu in Old Compton Street, later to go up in the world but then a shabby establishment where a great swatch of time might be spent over a coffee without challenge from the management. Occasionally in those purlieus one brushed against the modestly known, the modestly notorious, though if pressed for instances of the latter I could come up only with Ironfoot Jack, recalled recently by Anthony Powell's autobiography where though not named, he is accurately described as:

a man with a broadbrimmed black hat, long black coat, got up to look perhaps like The Sheriff in a Western. This effect, if aimed at, was diminished by one of his legs being shorter than the other, the short leg terminating in an appliance that looked rather like an iron door-scraper.

Anthony Powell goes on to give a good example of his characteristic permanent irascibility. He was the subject of an article in the *Evening Standard*, and later of a book, whether biography or autobiography I forget.

Of the Soho-haunters I really knew, Bloomsbury-dwellers in the main, a few have stayed in the mind. There was a genial girl familiarly called Ronnie, a form that somehow struck me, as did many trivial details of life in those days, as usable in my attempts at fiction: other possibilities arose at times. After I had gone back to Blackpool, a quiet, likeable, pock-marked girl-painter from New Zealand achieved, unlike Waller, extensive linage in the *Express* by keeping notes of the process as she gassed herself in her lodgings, the notes put in as evidence at the inquest. A young man called Paul, with a transatlantic accent, fair, quite good-looking though with teeth under attack, was the most amusing of this little group, the one I most liked to encounter, and seemingly with the biggest potential for fame. Surnames were not at all bandied about, and it was some time before I could be sure that Paul's was Potts, the obfuscating process perhaps increased by his own sense that Potts was a let-down after Paul (then, like Veronica, a less encountered Christian name than now), and quite unsuitable for a poet, which he was. I once showed him a poem of mine, possibly more, in the Coffee An', a big, unintimate, disagreeable café (a favourite of Iron-foot Jack's, no doubt because it gave him an extensive potential clientèle for his wares, pamphlets not patent medicines; though perhaps only the memory of the song my grandfather used to sing about "Medicine Jack" providing the latter association). Paul uttered a kind word about the verses ('beautiful', I seem to recall) but showed no greater interest than any poet in the manuscripts of his unpublished juniors.

I had ceased to know Paul before he was transformed in my apprehension to the sentimental, if left-wing, writer absolutely not to my taste, whose sparse books achieved attention from some critics because of their very badness (I think of his autobiographical volume entitled, ineffably, *Dante Called You Beatrice*). Those first years of the Thirties, before his talent had been disproved, must be classed as his golden age, however unlikely that might have seemed to him then.

Though I liked Soho, I saw that those of its denizens I knew were failures, perhaps permanently in that category, in which I did not put myself despite utter lack of literary success. I used to wonder, as the hours slipped away in the Bleu, just when the painters painted and the writers wrote, though the same question applied to me with even greater point. A fair slice of my day was spent at lectures at the law tutors, and the rest of it (the evenings, too, come to that) should have been devoted to reading for them. But I studied as spasmodically as I wrote verse or fiction. I was blessed (or cursed) with a brain usually capable of rapid comprehension of the printed word, and a dislike of not getting to the bottom of anything imparted by way of instruction. Instead of laying the foundation for becoming a really learned lawyer or prolific littérateur, I would listen to Red Nichols on the portable gramophone borrowed from Waller, or play the pin-table in Charley's.

The pin-table, incidentally, was nothing like the light-flashing, bell-ringing, vulgarly decorated and high-scoring machines of later years: it resembled more the old-fashioned Corinthian bagatelle board, and accurately judging the amount of pull-back required on the spring-loaded propelling piston could lead not only to getting the balls in the holes but also to getting a ball in the hole of its own colour, which then doubled the score for that particular hole, a refinement that added much interest. Charley offered twenty Players (then priced 11½d) if a certain score were attained or exceeded, and since only 1d was required to release the balls for play the odds were generous to those sacrificing their careers to become adept at the game. "What you want now is the double yellow," one would remark, as Waller, trench-coat open, sword-stick handle hooked on the glass top of the pin-table, pushed up his spectacles, and cautiously inched back the piston, risking his golden pudding. I say that, but at one period we were warned off the table by Charley for, he said, winning so many packets of Players as to hazard its profitability. It seems to me now that this ban may have been imposed less for the reason given than from Charley's irritation at being called from his steaming urn and other occupations behind the counter to check at the pin-table face that a winning score had been achieved, a nuisance exacerbated by Waller's manner of doing it (and he would also summon Charley when I was successful). The blank, owlish stare was belied by the complacent chortle in some such cry as: "Charley, Charley — another packet."

My two periods in London during my five years' articles, each for a two months' spell at the law tutors, Gibson and Weldon in Chancery Lane, were immediately before the Law Society's Intermediate Examination held in March 1931 and the Final in November 1933. As already made plain, the two periods have become in some degree conflated in my memory, though as I think about them I see they could be pretty well sorted out, probably with more explanation than they could bear, however.

London had previously been only the subject of a few brief visits, but I was soon on terms with it in 1931, at least the Soho, Bloomsbury, Chancery Lane axis; using the Underground a good deal. One stepped off the escalator with studied nonchalance; rather less easy to do than nowadays, since many escalators terminated not in the stair intermeshing with the floor and parallel to it, but in an oblique arrangement that required a positive alighting from the moving part. Down the subways one followed the appropriate colour of the guiding lights out of the corner of one's eye so as to conceal unfamiliarity. The subterranean wind seemed stronger, grittier, hotter, more aromatic in those days. No doubt one's hair was more unkempt, garments looser, flesh more sensitive. At Russell Square, the home station, a lift brought you up to seasons always milder than those of the north west, an effect enhanced by the frequent presence in the lift and the streets round about of studious Indians and Orientals. Doubling back along that curious part of Herbrand Street, almost a back alley (in which, nevertheless there was a pub, rather dim but occasionally visited), the straight macadam of Guilford Street was soon seen shining in the night rain. Or I might go direct to Charley's. Marchmont Street's modest shops and pubs (which in those days were still extant at the Bernard Street end, now ruined by foolish development), some of their habitués becoming familiar, offered almost a village ambience. Of my remembered experiences, I expect the more naive belong to the earlier stay, the more political to the later. As to the former, I once passed two respectable young girls in Southampton Row. Said one to the other, apropos an individual walking somewhat in front of me: "Just listen to that old man farting." The remark amended my innocent conception of the feminine. I often walked to Chancery Lane, usually via Lamb's Conduit Street and Red Lion Street, in the latter probably lingering at Charlie Lahr's bookshop. There were second-hand bookshops, too, in Chancery Lane, before one reached Gibson and Weldon's premises, No 27, though most were of the legal variety, regarded by me typically as boring.

Another axis (it just occurs to me) was partly formed by the Kingsway Tramway Subway, euphonious combination Marston, with his musical ear, liked to have on his lips. Did the tram come along Theobalds Road? Certainly it could be boarded at the top of Kingsway, and it then quite soon went below ground, emerging on the Embankment. There was at least one intermediate stop, round about Sardinia Street, involving (if, against the odds, one found it convenient to use) Piranesi-like staircases to the nether regions; regions now, of course, a one-way underpass for motor-cars from Waterloo Bridge to Holborn.

Though I occasionally used the Kingsway Tramway Subway with Waller and Marston, I expect on some pub crawl, it was the mode of my getting, alone, to the Old Vic, where I was quite a regular patron of the gallery, less frequently the more expensive pit. Five pence (old money) was the price of the ordinary doors gallery seat, that being a not over-generous length of backless, scrubbed, wooden bench, good preparation for the seating later normally supplied by the Navy. The early doors price, a few coppers more, usually ensured a seat on the front row or, preferably, the second, so as to avoid the brass rail along the gallery parapet spoiling one's line of sight. Opera and plays alternated, but whatever the programme the gallery held a fair proportion of local residents, some regulars, or otherwise known to each other, a few of proletarian eccentricity — an extension of the life of the market stalls in The Cut and Lower Marsh. The ambience, that quite short tram ride from the West End, took me back to Oldham days.

That the cultural aspirations of the poor, or not over well-off, paralleled what came more easily to the affluent seemed to me perfectly natural. Questions of élitism, of hating "bourgeois" culture, of a special brand of drama or poetry for the working-class did not arise; and even in later, Marxist days I imagined culture being desirably broadened as much by increased mass leisure and prosperity as by new forms and attitudes. Cruder (indeed, sillier) art for the "community" would have been a complete puzzlement. In Oldham, passing Garside Fold, as I often did as a boy — a court or little square of terraced cottages (by then a slum) characteristic of the housing accompanying factory building, a sort of secular cloisters — seeing the bare-footed and pantsless children, the slatternly women, I thought merely jobs with decent wages were required to bring learning as well as cleanliness into the deprived lives so painfully on view. Though there was an enigma that if the children were to stand eating jam "butties" at unseasonable hours, their parents ought to be able also to afford a cake of soap — even of "Monkey Brand" — I never doubted toiling humanity's essential goodness, its innate wish for advancement. That the latter was widespread among the lower classes was demonstrated, one might add, by conversations had and overheard during the ensuing war.

When I come across mentions of the Old Vic of those days, a good deal is, of course, recalled to mind. But under its own steam, memory brings back only two precise pictures. First, Charles Laughton as Lopakhin, waiting for the family's return — restless, sympathetic, intensely and appropriately Yorkshire petty bourgeois. Second, going twice to *The Magic Flute*, not known at all, nor really in those days my cup of tea; but I was imbued with the feeling that this, like some girl observed from afar, was a masterpiece I must get to know. In that epoch before the long-playing gramophone record, the business of grasping the shape of an extended musical work was difficult for one incapable of reading a score — the work in question seeming like some largely unmapped region, formless and extensive to a degree quite unimaginable once discs had made it familiar. I began to see *The Magic Flute's* shape, but its symbolism was not fully brought home perhaps because of the excessive modesty of the settings, almost on the lines of the gallery bench one was sitting on. Didn't I read the other day that the Tamino was Tudor Davies? Since I am not sure of that, no wonder further details of the Old Vic of 1931 have faded.

Re peregrinations, far-off girls, and the like, I had a constant sense of my personableness (though that is putting the thing too crudely, for certain regrets and self-criticisms were not absent), a narcissism that extended equally into the non-physical sphere. The pimples of adolescence accordingly caused me probably more than the usual distress. In my novel *The Perfect Fool* I have a page on this affliction so perhaps there is no need to expatiate much further. When at last, on my first London visit, my hair grew too long even for the poetic persona I was content to present, I went to a barber's shop in Southampton Row, quite a decent one, the assistant told me (it was a revelation, like discovering that wind could keep adults as well as babies awake) of the connection between acne and too infrequently washed hair. He also, with less impartial scientificalness, sold me a bottle of what then seemed expensive skin lotion, which I bore back to Guilford Street with hopes that were unfulfilled. As to remedies, in the end I and my brother (who came to suffer similarly, though not so acutely) used calomine lotion. I think it was he who started our referring to it affectionately as "pal o' mine". I was greatly impressed when I found he had his bottle made up with a *qs* of carbolic, at the suggestion of a chemist plainly sharing Hamlet's zeal for experimentation in the field. At one time (I believe when my mother owned a house overlooking Stanley Park, not far from the cricket ground) my brother and I, before finally going to bed, would sometimes appear with faces like the famous clown Doodles from the Blackpool Tower Circus or, more accurately, ghouls from European silent films, then still to be seen in a few small cinemas.

Going to a decent barber was not a mere quirk of London visits. The premier Blackpool saloon, Haslam's, I was taken to by my father in days of near infancy, when we were only holiday-makers in the town. Years later I renewed the practice on my own. When longer hair seemed desirable in my romantic view, I suppose visits were less frequent, and I expect I sometimes patronised places less grand (1s 6d was the considerable sum charged at Haslam's, I think doubled if one had a dry or wet shampoo). In fact, I once put myself in the hands of my friend Leslie's cousin (who had left Seafolde House prematurely to become a ladies' hairdresser) with instructions (similar to those given Lees about side roads, as recorded in *Souvenirs*) to eschew the clippers. But he used a dryer at random, making my locks look more abundant than even I cared for. At Haslam's I sometimes also had a face massage, about the same price as a haircut, with excellent effect on the complexion. After the hot towels, massage was effected with a pink substance that came off the face in dry little rolls, satisfyingly greyish: only when this plainly therapeutic process was completed was the visage anointed with an emollient preparation, followed by a cold towel or two. Afterwards, how glowingly one's image appeared in the barber's mirror!

Since my hair has gone on being thick and wavy, like my father's, its problems have remained. When I was called up in 1941 I still wore my hair long by the standards of those days; also I had a moustache. At the initial training establishment a visit to the barber (who would not have been taken on at Haslam's even to sweep up the hair) was part of the first day's routines. To the interest of the waiting fellow-conscripts, he ran his electrically-powered clippers not only up the back and sides but also over the moustache, leaving me to clear its undergrowth with my own razor. Of course, I realised it had to go, the moustached sailor being a Frog or banana republic concept alien to the R.N., but I wonder if one could have got the fellow to eschew, or at least temper, the clippers on the hair. Doubtful. News of the operation impressed my four-year-old son, who told those in Booth's Café and elsewhere enquiring about my fate in the Service that I had had this off and this off (pointing in turn to scalp and upper lip), and had to wash the cooks' clothes. The oddity of the last-named duty was an excusable error, perhaps due to the faulty orthography of the relevant letter home: an early chore was to wash the greasy cloths used by those transporting the great tins of food from the central galley to the peripheral messes.

A man's life might be written in terms of his hair-cuts (though possibly, like Prufrock measuring his with coffee spoons, only lives of a certain restrictedness would qualify). When at last I escaped from Blackpool and went to work in the Kent market and railway town of Ashford, my office looked out on the Ideal Hairdressing Saloon opposite, but I fancy it was for ladies only in those happy days before the "unisex" emporium. When later I joined the staff of the Woolwich Equitable Building Society I regularly used to go to the hairdressing department of the Royal Arsenal Co-operative Society, the other great non-profit-making organization of the place, but that was just after the war was over. In early London days my tonsorial experience could be called eclectic — witness a poem of the first year of the war, "The Barber", about having a hair-cut in the City.

I never found a truly satisfactory barber in London until in the Fifties I went to Michael's, off Haymarket; an establishment that on the whole lived up to its pretensions. Outside and on its unguents appeared the Imperial Russian Double Eagle, suggesting distinguished exiles usefully filling in time before counter-revolution restored them to their estates. One remarkable feature was that every customer had a card printed with two sides of a head (possibly the double-eagle logo had additional significance), each side being divided into sections, each section with a number indicating the length to which the hair in that section was to be cut (varying in the case of each customer). All the assistants cut to the same system; dividing the hair into the required sections as they proceeded, layering it with thinning scissors after cutting it to the length specified. The assistants were called by their fore-names, prefaced by "Mr". I had a good chap when I first went; then he left and I was assigned a young man I hoped would improve with experience among the phrenological cards and double eagles. Then, fulfilling an appointment, I found myself in the hands of Mr Philip, an assistant always noted with awe. He said my young man had been sacked for incompetence. That quality never showed itself in him. He must have been in his forties: plumpish; black, glistening hair, wavier than mine; formidable forearms, phenomenally hairy, revealed by the short-sleeved white jacket; the general effect that of a fashionable surgeon. As I sat swathed, seeing him in the mirror, I often speculated on the pattern of his life as he had revealed it in barberish converse, already set it seemed. He lived with his mother in the East End, plainly a Jewish mother's boy, though he had a long-established girl-friend whom he had no plans to marry. In my mind's eye I saw her like Nellie Gotliff, Issy's sister, spinster family friend of my youth — smart, hook-nosed, leanness in later years starting to wither. The truth to life of a popular song of those early days was brought home to me for the first time:

> Abie, Abie, Abie my boy, vat are ve vaiting for now?
> You promised to marry me von day in June;
> It's never too late and it's never too soon.
> All the family
> Keep on asking me:
> "Vich day, vat day?" I don't know vat to say.
> Abie, Abie, Abie my boy, vat are ve vaiting for now?

I quote from memory, and so have had to construct a stanzaic form. Since I remember the words so well the song was probably sung by the Happy Valley pierrots, whose performances I used to attend on a regular basis. The innocence of the Jewish comedy also surely places the song in the time before Hitler's rise.

Apart from my unexpressed memories of Jewish life, Mr Philip and I seemed to have nothing in common except soccer: he watched Clapton Orient, I Charlton Athletic. Eventually his ascerbic relationship with Michael came to an end, and I followed him to an emporium in an arcade between Piccadilly and Jermyn Street. One day, fulfilling my appointment at this place, the proprietor himself came to me and said: 'I'm afraid I have a shock for you.' Watching Orient at home the previous Saturday, Mr Philip had collapsed

37

and died. A perforated peptic ulcer was the cause — ulcers proving another unexpressed thing we had in common.

This must have been into the Sixties. Hair styles were changing: no more did the cap of hair, long but neatly fitting, seem desirable. An American actor called Dick Van Dyke appeared in a series popular on TV screens here: his hair, very short, brushed sideways rather than back, appealed to me as the effect to be achieved. In an article in some trendy magazine (perhaps read while waiting to be barbered by Mr Philip's indifferent successor) I saw a statement that the man of fashion had his hair cut by Chris of Wardour Street. At first I looked for ground floor premises displaying something akin to Michael's Tsarist insignia: in vain. Eventually I found Chris on a shabby first floor. It took a couple of visits to realise his assistants were no good, get myself in the hands of the maestro, who knew almost without my demonstrating what was required. His method was brilliant; always ending with a singe of fiery drama, remarked on one day by a young woman waiting for her husband. Chris, in his bad but effective English (he was Cypriot) briefly explained its beneficial effects. "Before he came to me he was bald," he told her seriously, indicating my still thick, if now short, hair, and leering at me surreptitiously in the glass. He himself had a black toupee, very soon pointing it out — "I have to wear it, you understand." With more business acumen and smarter premises, Chris's genius could have prospered, but I guess he was glad when he was enticed back to Cyprus by a salaried job in a hotel. Luckily, before he went he put me on to Jack — "I taught him all he know," said Chris, waggishly — a melancholy Italian, less dashing but of pretty well equal skill.

To return (not before time, it may be thought) to the anarchist bookseller and publisher Charlie Lahr (than whom there could have been no one less interested in getting his hair cut well), I was reminded of him not long ago by an excellent article by David Goodway in the *London Magazine* (Vol 17 No 2). Lahr's Red Lion Street shop had no glass on the outside, so that the books could be handled from the street. Putting a volume back on a shelf on one occasion, I accidentally pushed a few of its neighbours into the shop. Lahr, talking to a friend or customer inside, said in a voice I clearly heard: "What the hell's happening?" They were words that embarrassed me greatly, and whose impersonal complaint struck me as so effective that I have used the formula myself when the time might not have quite arrived for direct verbal attack on some trespasser to one's person or property. Lahr could see me through the gap between books and shelves, enlarged through my depredations, and I imagined myself for ever stigmatized in his view as a careless nitwit. In an instant he had picked up the the dislodged books, so there was nothing remedial I could do. I related this incident in a letter printed in a succeeding number of the *London Magazine*, and placed it, because of the feeling involved, in 1931, when I was nineteen, and gave 1933 as the time when I submitted two essays to Lahr for publication in his Blue Moon booklets series. It seems to me now the book-pushing episode could quite well have happened in 1933, for it was many a long year into manhood before I was able to cover up my gaucheries with a decent degree of charm and apology. The essays, too, may have been of a vintage slightly later than originally given, for they were full of gobbets of raw Marxism. But a letter came back from Lahr in which he said: "I would publish them if I wasn't broke." Bitter-sweet words! I had published scarcely anything at that date, was madly keen to do so, and his response was one of the few positive ones I had ever had to my numerous submissions.

Like other characters quite often to be seen about, such as Iron-foot Jack and a young right-wing poet in a red cloak with hair down his back who called himself, possibly with justification, Count Geoffrey Potocki de Montalk, Charlie Lahr had achieved a degree of fame or notoriety. He used to pass on his bicycle, his feet in sandals in all weathers, a strange feature being that his big-toe nails were small and embedded in ample surrounding cushions of flesh. Not until I went to Africa during the war, and saw the big-toes on display there, did I realise that this was a result of going shoeless.

I had a strong wish to gaze on the admired and famous, no doubt a pretty universal trait, but surely most marked in the restless provincial. At this epoch I once saw Aldous Huxley in St James's Square (possibly coming from the London Library, I realise now), and followed him into Straker's, a stationer's in the Haymarket, long vanished. There he picked up from the counter, the more closely to examine it, a grotesquely large cardboard model of a lead-pencil tip, made for advertising display purposes. For some time after, I scanned his work for mention of this, a typical image of his earlier writing, not really kept up, alas. He was wearing a nice tweed suit, a plain orange tie (not then to be found in ordinary shops), and carrying a copy of the Phoenix Library edition (cheap hardback) of *Crome Yellow*, needless identification, for despite the absence of TV, still to be made available if not actually invented, he was immediately recognizable. I myself bought nothing in Straker's: probably, if accosted by an assistant, went out with some slight mime, convincing to myself, of having left my wallet at home or of being taken short — needless elaborations of the shy.

Of course, a different world was entered stepping into 27 Chancery Lane. Gibson and Weldon had started as an ordinary firm of solicitors, taken on law tutoring for articled clerks perhaps as an adjunct to its London agency work for provincial firms, then found the tutoring side grow to become virtually a separate enterprise. The cramming was carried on with great skill, the two-months' course a swift but intensive revision of the entire syllabus, culminating, just before the examination, in a test under examination conditions. The results of this were posted — dread proclamation! — the course members bracketed in such categories as "Will pass", "May pass", and ending with a few varying degrees of hopelessness, speculating on divine intervention and suchlike facetiae.

The lecturers were solicitors: most had been in ordinary practice; all were adept at forecasting the examination questions. One of them, L. Crispin Warmington, some elderly solicitors will still remember. Like Aldous Huxley, he wore tweeds and a soft collar, but was plump, not etiolated. He lectured on tort, perhaps contract as well, in a relaxed and extremely leisurely style, making a good few funny jokes. "I am strolling in my garden in Esher before dinner," he would begin, retailing a few circumstantial details not of strict relevance. Then a bough from a neighbour's tree falls on his head, or noxious fumes drift in from other property. The picture conjured up (particularly by the susurrating syllables "Esher", a place known by name but never visited, Warmington's utterance throwing new light on their pronunciation) was of a gracious way of life, far from that implied by a Blackpool clientèle of "spec" builders and boarding-house landladies.

Normally, the nomenclature of the land, in fictional examples illustrating the law relating to it, was Blackacre and Whiteacre (the connotation of great estates perhaps a hangover from days when small owners of freeholds were less common). Two names were usually enough — in relation to rights and obligations annexed to the property, for instance — though a Greenacre might sometimes have to be imported. I believe it was Warmington, moving away from his Surrey neighbours, who introduced such exotica as Purpleacre, a usage I took up eagerly in answering test questions, even examination questions; proceeding straight to such concepts as Puceacre without first exhausting the restrained palette, a good example of the pointless show-off side of my nature, also illustrated by my choice of pseudonyms for labelling test papers — Panurge, Stephen Dedalus, and the like. The American film actor, Edward Everett Horton, called his Californian Estate Belly Acres, a jest I would certainly have taken as mine had I known of it then.

There had, of course, been more or less boring codifications, such as the Sale of Goods Act and the Bills of Exchange Act, but it seems in retrospect that the subjects of my student days were still dominated by the common law, the great leading cases about the escape from property of dangerous substances; snails in ginger-beer bottles; advertisements guaranteeing the efficacy of influenza remedies. Though I came into the law at an awkward moment so far as real property was concerned, the old law having to be learnt as well as the 1925 property statutes, by comparison with later developments I enjoyed the last glow of a golden age. Parliament had not yet become maniacal in its statute-making activities; the war had still to come that was to give such an amazing fillip to government by statutory rules and orders (already the subject of foreboding by some who had found sinister the comparatively modest effects in that area of the 1914–18 war). Before my call-up in April 1941, I was already used to a mass of law being contained in pages ever-changing (but ever-accumulating) between loose-leaf binders. For the Law Society's examinations in the early Thirties, books could be safely read in editions of leisurely obsolescence, and certain fluid topics, like tax law, were actually excluded from the syllabus. Nevertheless, the examinations were a burden, notorious obstacles, flooring quite a few who aspired to be solicitors, some of them condemned to an unqualified (and even embittered) life in the law, like the character F. S. Shaw later appearing in these pages. The failure rate in the Intermediate could exceed 40%; for the Final not greatly less — so even placed in the "Will pass" category, as I was on both occasions, anxiety persisted until the results came through. Towards the end of my articles I resolved never again to study for an examination, being cheesed-off with the unceasing routine that had started with the Oxford Junior Locals (the "O-levels" of the time) some seven years before. Little did I imagine that as I turned into my thirties I should once again spend long months being examined in fields of learning to which I was fundamentally indifferent.

The question arises here, as it did in *Souvenirs* apropos confining one's running prowess to contests over short distances (and as it might in some celestial school report), as to lack of energy, application, genius. For the Law Society's Final the Honours papers were separate, taken a week after the Pass examination. I had decided initially Honours were beyond the notch I was prepared to stretch myself to; had no enthusiasm, any way, to sit for them: besides, I was reluctant to be longer parted, even for a week, from my wife-to-be. But it was borne in on me that most of the finalists studying at Gibson's were dimmer than I, a lesson somehow not carried over from the Intermediate course, or other events in my life where such comparisons were possible. Eventually I went to some authority at Gibson's (I expect with inward quaking and after much courage-screwing) to try to enter for the Honours examination after all, but it was too late, even to pay the late fee. Acquisition of Honours meant nothing in the business of being a solicitor, but might have told when it came to seeking jobs — and therefore changed my life.

Anxiety to reach another, happier state of existence (such as being united with the loved one) raises another perhaps more universal question; namely, the characteristic life possesses of compelling one to waste it. Or, if that is putting the thing in terms too extreme, the sense at almost every stage of life that the present is a mere preliminary to true happiness or fulfilment, a time to be passed, occasionally stoically endured or frittered away. I advanced this business in a poem once — man's squandering of his most precious substance — but have failed to turn up the lines. It was acutest during the war, as I shall come to again, but it showed its power during my two London sojourns. Indeed, it could be said that the purgatorial state of being an articled clerk (and a schoolboy, too, for that matter) was designed to keep one's eye on some Nirvana ahead, no doubt a ploy of the bourgeois ethic and the strategy of its dominance. The matter was well put in a song of the day, though the singer perhaps places the emphasis on his own misfortunes or deficiencies:

> My life is only a vamp till ready,
> I've played the long introduction thro'.
> How much longer must I wait
> For the orchestral leader to give me the cue?

This excellent song was made familiar to me, I think in the

period immediately following my Final, by Marston, who sang it both away from and at the piano. The words were by Clark Gibson, a forgotten name now; the music by Fred Elizalde, a remarkable musician who needs, I believe I am right in saying, to be rediscovered. Marston may not have known that Elizalde was also a composer of "classical" works, including a violin concerto, but it would be unfair not to credit him with a considerable nose for the good and the unusual. It did not need him, as readers of *Souvenirs* will know, to introduce me to the music hall, but he revealed that one could stand at the rear and sides of the stalls (probably the dress circle, too) at the Holborn Empire for half-a-crown, may have been two shillings. Obliquely across the great, gently sloping upland of heads and shoulders I see in my mind's eye the figure of Billy Bennett ("Almost a gentleman" the subtitle of his billing) in tails, with a dicky apt to curl up and escape from his low-cut waistcoat; hair in a quiff — perhaps not awfully unlike in appearance and attitudes his namesake Arnold, risen rather more convincingly from the petty bourgeoisie. I recently came across a specimen of the rhyming couplets recited by Billy Bennett as the climax of his act, and wish I had copied them out: still funny, they seemed to me, and antici-pating by a few years the surrealism that was to appeal quite a lot to English intellectuals when it crossed the Channel. His patter usually had to do with physical deformities of family and friends, like that of the contemporary comedian Les Dawson. "He had a wart on the back of his neck," said Bennett, "so big he used to button his collar on it." After the war the fine comedian Jimmy Wheeler continued this appealing tradition, though his material also concerned human ailments, e.g. he goes to the doctor with a boil on his nose, which the doctor taps with a medical hammer. "Does that hurt?" "Yes." "I thought it would."

It was sometimes possible at the Holborn Empire, though having only paid the standing charge, surreptitiously to occupy a vacant seat, in my case with guilty unease. The trespass was safest after the main turn in the second half, when some seat-holders left for good. What probably remained to be seen in sudden comfort was an acrobatic or juggling act, perhaps two men who called themselves the Haekenschmidt Brothers (or Twins), the climax of whose performance was to wrestle in slow motion, the snail's pace of the convolutions involving enormous but unostentatious strength, the cinema illusion enhanced by the pair being lit only by a flickering spot. I sometimes wonder if I saw at that time two tap-dancers, man and wife, regulars at the Lewisham Hippodrome and New Cross Empire after the war, when certainly they were getting on in years. Come to think of it, though, they were more an opening than a closing turn. The climax of *their* act was the man assuming a succession of characters while still dancing. Truth to tell, the differentiation was not great, a drawback countered by the nature of the characterization being announced before being carried out. Some of these phrases became family sayings; one of them, "Old man crossing the road", once used when driving in the car, now getting fresh laughs through its personal pedestrian application.

Neither Marston nor Waller lasted the pace in London. (No boast is implied about my own toughness. I had one of my tonsillitis attacks, and my mother came down, worried about me. I had moved into an attic room, I think at Waller's suggestion as being a great bargain — perhaps it had been occupied by him before his feud with the landlady. The small saving in money was scarcely relevant, though probably the sloping ceilings, and commodiousness, appealed to me. On seeing it, my mother was appalled: far from finding it agreeably reminiscent of *La Bohème,* she described it to my brother as being like the *mise-en-scène* of *The Rat,* a play and film of the age in which Ivor Novello played the eponymous hero (or villain), an Apache, in the hooligan of Paris sense). Waller contracted TB; Marston some less definable ailment. Against the odds, the latter returned to the family house in Blackpool, worked in his father's business.

Councillor Marston was a genial man, steel-grey hair greased and brushed back, a cigarette ever between his lips — which nevertheless did not prevent him from being as talkative as his younger son. The elder son had already married, left home, though I got to know him slightly, even playing bridge with him, as did my brother. He lacked his brother's self-confidence, his character indicated by words he often employed when embarking on trying to make his contract at the bridge-table, as my brother soon pointed out to me: "This is insuperably difficult, partner" — another phrase that passed into *Coterie-sprache.* His wife was good-looking, though (to be ungallant) not so good-looking as her younger sister, chiselled-featured, pale-blue-eyed, with whom Marston himself was then involved. This girl had long been noted by the articled clerks at Wylie Kay's, for she worked nearby. On meeting Marston again, in his Blackpool milieu, it was initially an agreeable if tantalizing frisson, rather like standing next to Aldous Huxley in Straker's, to find myself cutting the cards for her.

The Marston house was an ordinary modern suburban house, though commodious, even running to a room that housed a half-size billiards table. The passage to the room was impeded by a number of large cardboard cartons, which proved to contain packets of Kensitas cigarettes, bought by Councillor Marston wholesale, though I suspect his motivation was less the saving of money than having at hand a store of fuel for his inordinate consumption, plus the pleasure of accumulating, in advance thereof, the gift-coupons then to be found in Kensitas packets. I sometimes accepted a Kensitas from Councillor Marston, but marvelled at anyone smoking the things, even allowing for the gifts. My own taste, moving from my mother's Craven A through such exotica as Abdulla brown-paper Russian blend and Wills's oval, though Virginia, Passing Cloud, had probably already settled down with Player's Gold Leaf, then untipped, sold in tin boxes containing twenty-four cigarettes at 1s. 5d., coffin nails of real excellence.

There was a free and easy air in the Marston house, despite the domestic bind to be mentioned. Marston's quick, if not profound, grasp of public issues enabled him to trade opinions with his father on local as well as national affairs. The Councillor was by no means averse to skirting the cartons and having a game of fifty up, a performer in the adroit family class — a Gaev. Pots of tea, sometimes food, were to be had at irregular times, and late hours were kept — a bridge four of Marston and his girl, me and my future wife, once going on, at Marston's persuasion, till dawn; debauched life for our kind of provincial society, though only tea was drunk. Marston's mother occasionally appeared, to be typically treated by him with ostentatious endearments (not precluding genuine affection, however), disarming (though not necessarily designed to do so) any outsider suspecting strains in the household. Was Mrs Marston on the bottle, or a touch like the receiver of the pigs' broadcasts? At any rate, her vagueness and largely off-stage existence were useful years later when I had to invent a wife for the villain of *The Second Curtain*.

It was not unknown in the town that Councillor Marston was involved with another lady; visited her at her house. One evening, a good deal later than the marathon bridge-playing period, I saw him across a hotel lounge, too far away to be obliged to greet him. He was sitting at a table with a person in a fur coat. My companion told me this was the lady of the long-standing liaison. In those days of my still essentially romantic view of life, I was amazed: the lady was far from young, and less superficially attractive than Mrs Marston. Going from wife to mistress — it was like the gag of the comedian Michael Bentine when his black hair was particularly upstanding. "Don't worry about my hair," he would advise the audience, "it's only a wig." And to prove it he would indeed remove a wig, only to reveal his own equally, if not more, abundant hair beneath.

Waller's TB merely punctuated his London life: he returned to Blackpool to live not until some years after the war; an even more surprising example of the Dixie syndrome. I had the details of his illness only in retrospect, being out of touch with him at the critical time. The case was grave, involving at one stage an artificial pneumothorax, which nevertheless did not allow the infected lung to heal. Needless to say, Waller personalised the disease in characteristic manner. He said once he woke out of a doze in hospital to find a clergyman at his bedside, perhaps even muttering some *nunc dimittis* over him. For the first time he realised his death was anticipated, resolved there and then to postpone that fate; as an initial step telling the cleric to bugger off. An unofficial, probably herbal, remedy for comsumption called (if I have the spelling right) UMKALOBO had been achieving publicity for its efficiency, perhaps in the *Daily Express*, despite the connotation of witch-doctoring in its name. Waller commanded his parents to obtain a supply, took it as directed, and was quite rapidly cured. It may be that his old faith in the power of the human body to dispel unsuitable invaders helped the process.

In writing of the past, how far should one anticipate the future? The question is partly artistic, for of course the focal distance changes the picture. Does truth come into it? That is another naive question. The later destinies of Waller and Marston, known to me increasingly mainly through hearsay, were strange, not least in the matrimonial sphere. I feel it would not be right to indicate them at this point.

Everybody knows that whatever thread or scene of life is isolated, contemplated, more remains that impinges and would add richness and complication. It will be plain that the selections offered here are those filtered through largely unprompted memory and a writer's variable energy and power. Sometimes I have tried to discover dates and sequences when the chronology of memory struck me as

46

especially unsound. But to have had to deal with the actual raw material of the times would have added enigma to the narrative — names, motives, allusions, faded; footnotes on footnotes required — though one regrets the loss of subtlety and complication. Besides, Proustian length would have been involved, Proustian genius lacking.

4   The Loose Group

How being miserable for myself I began,
And now am miserable for the mass of man.

— George Barker

In the train on my way back to Blackpool after my first spell at
Gibson and Weldon's in 1931, passing along the side corridor, I
saw in a compartment some prominent members of the New Party,
then recently founded by Sir Oswald Mosley after his break from
the Labour Party, that being prompted by frustration at the impo-
tence of its policies about unemployment and so forth. I lingered
outside the compartment, in the manner of my sleuthing of Aldous
Huxley. Eventually, Harold Nicolson emerged. Somehow the
opportunity came for me to tell him I had been at the Party's big
meeting of a few days before, when Lady Cynthia Mosley (as I had
written in a letter or lost journal: the awful phrase unforgotten)
had "bared her bosom to the mob", a reference to the slightly
low-cut black dress worn by the attractive speaker and the heckling
by the left-wing slice of the audience. The meeting could well have
been that actually launching the New Party, which Sir Oswald
could not attend through illness, and from which W. J. Brown
apparently ratted.

In the first volume of Harold Nicolson's *Diaries and Letters* there
is an entry about his going by train to Manchester on 27 April, but
I feel my brief encounter was earlier than this, some time in March.
I can't recall what, if any, item of political news or wisdom was
imparted by Nicolson, but he did momentarily pinch my sleeveless
pullover (worn under a jacket) between finger and thumb, and say:
"I like your sweater." It was in fact unusual for those days, being

red — a nineteenth birthday present from my wife-to-be, who had searched for it long and far. Of course, I knew Nicolson was married to Victoria Sackville-West and guessed of his preferred sexual proclivities no more than any other member of the public, even after his display of interest in a young man's garb — after which, I may say, he soon passed on. Though as I write these words it occurs to me for the first time that his coming out of the compartment at all may have been motivated by my presence in the corridor; behaviour prompted by the chance of erotic adventure being as foolish as that prompted by the chance of charismatic encounter.

I was so politically green that though I saw the Labour Party might not be best pleased at the defection of one of its most prominent members, I could not understand the fury of the left opposition to Mosley's New Party. Its dynamic had rapid consequences, however. My own disillusionment came when, quite soon, the Party gave birth to sections with joined abbreviations or, perhaps, acronyms: ORGACT (as it might be: I forget the actuality — though Nicolson's book reminds me that the party itself came to call itself NUPA). My objection was initially almost an aesthetic one, not seeing the fascist parallel; simply feeling that this patent medicine nomenclature and quasi-militarism would not do for me, nor for the English generally. No doubt the proper penny dropped quickly thereafter: certainly in a year or so NUPA had become BUF, the British Union of Fascists, and when I was in London in 1933, once again at Gibson and Weldon, the comparatively moderate heckling of the Conway Hall (or wherever that meeting I attended was) had turned into the protesting crowds outside the Mosley Rally at the Albert Hall, the hooves of the police horses sliding on the polished pavements, the fresh horse-droppings bright against the dark grey. Was I with Marston on this occasion, or had he already joined commercial forces with the Councillor? Someone was with me, perhaps Waller. It was possible, to avoid the police break-up of the mob, to go farther up Kensington Gore, board a bus, and ride past the Albert Hall; the slow progress through the disorder enabling anti-fascist protestations to be shouted through the windows of the upper deck — a cowardly procedure that suited my fear of being bonked, or ridden down, by the Cossacks.

In Blackpool, between my two London sojourns, I became active in local left-wing politics, such as they were. I recall being with both Marston and Waller when I said that for my part I was ready to join the Communist Party of Great Britain. That was after

Marston's return to the family house, though perhaps the cause merely his temporary ill-health. With typical enterprise he had made contact with a small discussion group that at that time met weekly in some upper room, I think of a pub. As at J. Isaacs's seminar, I actually spoke on my first attendance — some mainly D. H. Lawrentian tripe about righting social injustice by personal integrity. A man called Warnock gave out some ideas about class rule through the apparatus of police and army from Lenin's *State and Revolution*. I was immediately profoundly convinced by this theory of the State (as I was, probably a little later, about the Oedipus Complex), and started to read the Marxist classics. It shows the strength of the tide that one was in left-wing politics before one had read them to any appreciable extent.

Terry Warnock was one of the few men I have known whose views and proposals for action almost invariably seemed correct, or at any rate hard to controvert. Another who comes to mind (though in the realm of business) was an executive of the Woolwich Equitable Building Society I worked closely with during my last years there as solicitor. Oddly enough (or perhaps not so oddly, since thirty years or so separated my association with the diverse pair), George Swainsbury was a man of the independent, unorthodox right; Warnock's leftism, at least during the few years I knew him, orthodox CPGB. Terry — smallish, lean, strong nose, weathered face, wide, turned-down mouth, straight black hair starting to be grey-streaked, in his forties; not utterly unlike the actor Claude Rains — had come from the North-East, at that time blighted by unemployment. He was really an engineering fitter, but in Blackpool had to work as a labourer in the Corporation gas department. I was haunted by what he casually told me, that a day of digging trenches left him so exhausted that mental work after it was virtually impossible. He had a small socialist library on the dresser top in the kitchen, including a book by the Italian Labriola, who I suppose later in the Stalinist epoch would have been considered heretical. I write this having just read a biography of Ernst Mach (who was lambasted by Lenin in *Materialism and Empirio-Criticism*, a work also ploughed through by me in those days), which mentions the nineteenth century socialist theoretician Josef Dietzgen, name not come across since the time of which I am writing. Whether Terry also had a book of his I do not recall (I write "a book", but I think only one would have been possible — *The Positive Outcome of Philosophy*, title that has stuck). Certainly Dietzgen's name was on the lips of the SPGB members soon to be mentioned. Typical of Lenin's methods that nothing of Mach's greatness or even interest comes through the polemic. I daresay Terry's power derived from a similar narrow intensity. Later in the decade, the writings of the communist forefathers became more easily available (not Labriola and Dietzgen, however), but most of Terry's books had come from America, cheap editions of Wobbly days. Amazing works — of Victorian confidence and *fin de siècle* sedition.

Mrs Terry (as Marston always referred to her, exercising his charm as ever in female company, most finding it agreeable) took in the odd visitor during the summer season, probably just for bed and breakfast, proving beyond doubt the advantage of their having migrated from Tyneside. She was pale, energetic, quite a match for her husband, sang in the premier local choral society. A picture returns of her arriving home after a rehearsal, dropping her score of *The Creation* (or whatever) on the kitchen table; making tea for the two or three of us who had been gassing and smoking with Terry round the aforesaid table; providing a plate of biscuits. The ambience was undoubtedly working-class, yet not far from some atmosphere of ancient days of my own — for instance, my great-aunt Polly's household, touched on in *Souvenirs*. Still, there is (or was) a gap between the petty bourgeoisie (however impoverished) and the working-class (however cultivated); made even more apparent to me in the Navy during the war.

The home of at least one other Blackpool CPGB member was nearer to those mean dwellings glimpsed in Garside Fold in the Oldham of my boyhood — that of a hulking, slapdash young woman, with small children, where meetings sometimes took place. This must have been the setting of a poem from the notebook to be described later (in self-defence I quote no more than three lines):

> The small, crowded room, the wallpaper
> burgeoning faded roses and the table groaning
> with elbows, DAILY WORKERS, cigarette ends . . .

I was easier with the petty bourgeoisie than with the proletariat; mainly a matter of shared culture, for, man to man, personal inhibitions held sway. I wonder whether a good deal of the working-class culture celebrated by Richard Hoggart in *The Uses of Literacy* (a work of illusion, any way), is not properly petty bourgeois culture. After the war, when the working-class became

51

relatively prosperous, it showed itself remarkably vulnerable to culture of an imposed, commercial, Tin Pan Alley kind; a result the Thirties did not anticipate. In a fascinating contribution to *Of Books and Humankind*, the volume of essays and poems presented to Bonamy Dobrée in 1964, Richard Hoggart (at the time of which he was writing undergraduate to Dobrée's professorship at Leeds) tells of the latter buying a cake at a "bad cheap shop" which would have been immediately recognizable as such by the respectable poor. I would say, rather, by the discriminating petty bourgeoisie, for it is the working-class, simply through numbers if nothing else, that has allowed so many bad cheap things to flourish. The sort of cultural plus that appeals to Hoggart — home-baked cakes and bread being typical — seems to me not of working-class persistence at all; certainly not among urban proletarians: as related in *Souvenirs*, when my grandmother ran out of bread she rather guiltily sent to the nearest corner shop in Hollins Road for a loaf of the kind bought by most of the working-class every day of their lives if they could afford it (and usually rather a good article in the North of England of the Twenties). However, in matters of class it does not do to be too dogmatic.

A knotty problem of political tactics, or more enduring political attitude, was often decided by Terry cutting across argument by beginning a succinct account of the issues involved and the action needed with a Leninlike: "What is the situation, comrades?" — a phrase that removed from his awesome presence came to be used in more trivial areas of life. There was little call for demagoguery in the tiny parties of the town to the left of the Labour Party, but I doubt if Terry would in any event have been effective as a rabble-rouser. Such few and faint opportunities for exercising that role were best left to the local leader of the CPGB, Ben Goodman. He was a big, dark, friendly, fluent man, working-class, like Terry; attractive to women; not old, though balding; said to settle matters of party tactics not with Terry's ratiocination but as a fraction of two, in bed with a woman comrade. Ben was always solicitous (no wonder he appealed to the ladies) about the tasks I could possibly handle, given my status as embryo solicitor. I stood in the street on a few Saturdays, selling "Dailies" (*The Daily Worker*, now *The Morning Star*), but Ben was happier when I was writing for the paper, which I did once or twice about the problems of the seasonal worker, particularly as to unemployment benefit, law being much involved.

There seemed no incongruity between the large aims that had led one into politics (internationalism, anti-fascism, protection of the Soviet Union against a renewal of the post-Revolution interventionist war, distributing work, wealth and art more equitably) and the chores and arguments of local affairs — though even that phrase is a bit too grandiose for the preoccupations then of small provincial left-wing parties. The day to day detail and atmosphere of such activities are wonderfully recaptured in Edward Upward's trilogy, *The Spiral Ascent*, though I myself lacked the sensitivity and dedication of Upward's hero, Alan Sebrill, and so never felt as truly excruciating the conflict between political work and the poetic life, virtually dropping out of politics (one cannot say painlessly, but without sleepless nights) after a few years of pretty close involvement. Moving from Blackpool, I moved also from political friends and routines, and failed to re-acquire them. Then the war came, with the inevitability of being called up, and that seemed a substitute for political action, or at any rate a salve for one's guilt at political inactivity. I suppose in a sense I suffered from the Sebrill syndrome, but it was rather subsumed in what much later I would have tagged the Wallace Stevens syndrome. The life of contemplation (a phrase, a notion, which then I shouldn't have been able even to formulate about myself; indeed, I think I picked it up from something John Lehmann wrote long afterwards) was what I was best suited for. Day to day life in society (inescapable even in a "life of contemplation", unless one takes the veil!) was, of course, dominated by my continuing occupation as a lawyer. Progress in that, like my political side, suffered from pusillanimity, weakness, lack of real interest in making a name or even money on that side of life. Eventually I found a legal job that suited such talents as I possessed, and rather late in my career I blossomed with the job — the lateness being lucky, for earlier success would have left me with even less time and élan for writing. I really recognized almost from the start that I should never abandon a "job" in favour of "writing", for I never felt the least confidence in being able to attract an audience, even for a book review. Besides, there was my native indolence, already sufficiently indicated.

About the simplest political matters I was at first totally ignorant. The mechanics of chairing a meeting — such as the proper way of putting a resolution and its amendments — caused some worry, even apropos the small friendly meeting it might befall me to have the conduct of. It would have been more to the point if L. Crispin

Warmington had expatiated on these matters instead of the rule in *Rylands v. Fletcher*. What was the Trades Council, often mentioned? What were the full names of the trades unions referred to by various initials and acronyms? Classes and publications and media courses on such things then scarcely existed. I could not avoid being brought on by all I was involved in.

By the time of the General Election of 1935 I was able with outward sangfroid to chair a large meeting in the Co-operative Hall under the auspices of the local branch of the "Peace Council", a popular front organization which might have been invented for a left-winger leading a respectable bourgeois existence; in a sense was! All three candidates for the Blackpool constituency — Conservative, Liberal, Labour — had been invited by the Peace Council to come on a common platform to put their views on keeping the peace (or, rather, restoring it, for it was the time of Mussolini's invasion of Abyssinia). In the end none had dared refuse. The audience was preponderantly left. The turn-out, the heckling, the publicity, presumably advanced the cause of peace; the cause of the Peace Council, at any rate. When the proceedings terminated there was a moment of farce. The Conservative candidate, J. Roland Robinson, barrister son of a local solicitor, next to me on the platform, asked me to lead the meeting in the singing of the National Anthem. I was horrified. Such a manifestation of nationalism would be a negation of the meeting's purpose; besides, what on earth would such as Terry Warnock (no doubt among the audience) think of my being involved in the patriotic cliché? On the spur of the moment I made a stilted riposte: rather characteristic, I see now — "That is not on the meeting's agenda." I wanted to imply that the other candidates might have scruples, as well as myself: it had been quite a triumph of negotiation to get them all three to appear simultaneously and to agree a procedure. Though the legal touch to this reply might be thought to have held some appeal for him, Mr Robinson did not bandy words further, but raised his voice in song, in which he was quickly joined by a sufficient number. I stood in agonized silent embarrassment.

As expected, Mr Robinson got in, and in fact represented the town until 1964 when he was appointed Governor of Bermuda, and enobled as Lord Martonmere. One sometimes saw his by then substantial figure, surmounted by tropical-breeze-blown white plumes, in newsreels or newspaper photographs. The imposing name chosen for his barony must have been that of some Blackpool lacustrine feature, long vanished; the first part of the name, Marton, surviving as that of a somewhat decayed district not far, in fact, from the eccentric Marston ménage.

Contemporaneously with writing these occasionally facetious words, I have been reading Thomas Okey's *A Basketful of Memories*, published in 1930. In this autobiographical sketch, Okey looks back to the ideological side of his youth:

> It is difficult to convey to the present age the enthusiasm of the 'sixties and 'seventies of the last century for the new gospel heralded by the names of Darwin and Herbert Spencer — a feeling akin to that of religious emotion — a feeling expressed in lyric form by Thomas Hardy:
>
> > In the 'seventies I was bearing in my breast,
> > > Penned tight,
> > Certain starry thoughts that threw a magic light
> > On the workhouse and the soundless hours of rest,
> > In the 'seventies, aye! I bore them in my heart
> > > Penned tight.
>
> We felt that we were working for a "something" not ourselves that made for right thinking, a *Vita Nuova* for humanity.

This, or something like it, could be said of the early nineteen-thirties. Later in the decade spots of doubt appeared — not about internationalism or equal social opportunity, nor requiring from believers cover-ups or hypocrisy. It was mainly the sense that the Wordsworthian bliss had gone, that the world would have to be re-made by fallible men, rather than ideas and ideals transforming the individual as well as society.

Poems of mine began to appear in periodicals in 1934, but I think the only piece containing any straightforward political idealism is the "sections from a longer work" published in the Spring 1937 number of *New Writing*, which refers to the "smiling moustaches" of Stalin and of the then leader of the American Communist Party, Earl Browder (later in trouble, and disgraced). The phrase sticks in the mind as something one would prefer not to be on record, but there may be other, forgotten, embarrassments. Parts of the poem were influenced by Stephen Spender's long poem, *Vienna*, so may have been written in 1934 or 1935. In my first book of verse, published in January 1939 (I let this date stand for the moment) political notions are masked — undeliberately — by surrealism, Gravesian (perhaps I should say Ridingesque) anecdote, and general obfuscation. (When printing the smiling moustaches poem, John Lehmann — I blame him not — left out what may have been the best part of the thing: some prose rather like Section III of Auden's *The Orators*). Between the "beautiful" poetry, like the specimen shown to Paul Potts, and the poems in the second half of the Thirties more or less acceptable to the editors of little magazines, I wrote some proletarian or at any rate "proletcult" poems, most of which I believe are extant still, in a trunk in the loft above me as I write. I wonder whether I ought not to find them before ending my account of these times, whether anything faintly interesting could be made of them, even if only in the egg-on-the-smiling-moustaches department.

The discussion group to which Marston took me was not utterly removed from the *mise-en-scène* of the short story, "Sunday", by Edward Upward, which appeared in the then dazzling, still fascinating, anthology *New Country* (1933). At my suggestion, my brother requested this as one of the books for a book prize he won in his last year at school in the Isle of Man. My first reading of the book may well have been of his copy, the arms of the school in gilt on the front binding, like *Fanny Hill* in brown-paper covers. The Upward story, however, ends with a prognostication rather too solemn to correspond to the Blackpool step forward. The first person narration of the story's start changes to "you" for a discussion of the force of history, and then, for the commitment to left-wing action, to the third person; the famous key sentence being: "He will go to the small club behind the Geisha Café." Quite soon the Blackpool group grew and broadened, and met in premises less conspiratorial than the original upper room.

I believe the notion of the "loose group" has its origin in the tactics of the Socialist Party of Great Britain ("SPGB"), to be used where political consciousness is rudimentary or ill-spread. In all events, the phrase was first heard on the lips of John Hill who, with an older man, Sammy — amazingly the passage of time has deleted his surname from remembrance — were the two sole Blackpool members of that tiny and simon-pure Marxist party. Sammy owned a snack-bar (as it may well have been called even in those days) in the part of the town patronised by the humblest visitors, hot pies and mushy peas being the kinds of item available, edible enough though the quality would probably have been deplored by Hoggart. Sammy was benevolent but unremarkable save for his beliefs. I never knew him well: I think he was rather a slave of the snack-bar. John Hill became, perhaps always was, chairman of the group. The snack-bar seemed not to prevent *his* assiduous attendance. Perhaps he only helped there in the "season", or attended the group on his night off. It was an odd sensation (in spite of his theoretical association with dinners, shortly to be mentioned), going to the snack-bar for the first time, to see John in professional white apron taking pies and peas to the untableclothed tables, bringing one's own order, in fact, since he was a youngish, attractive, middle-class intellectual. Alas, his day was already over, maybe had never properly dawned. In indifferent health, separated from his wife, he lived alone in mediocre digs. Because he applied his Marxism to cultural as well as economic and political matters all he had to say interested me. In early days I was struck and convinced by his delineation of the labour theory of value, using "dinner" as the unit of wages — a dinner per day being sufficient to sustain a worker and allow him to reproduce himself. "A man earns ten dinners a week . . ." It should be said that the General Election of 1935 cast him in a new, rather impressive part — temporary assistant Labour Party Agent. Going into the Committee Rooms to address envelopes, one found him at a desk, in authority — as odd a sensation as originally discovering him as a waiter.

But really my sense of what he was, in calibre and character, has faded to a shade with the years. He was strongest in the field of music, may possibly have been a professional in some aspect of it, though his views might seem quaint if accurately recalled now. I myself often uttered the simplistic notion that *Gurrelieder* was symptomatic of bourgeois cultural decline, on the grounds of its gargantuan scale, and forces required to perform it, including an iron chain. The notion of examining the later, twelve-tone Schoenberg from some such standpoint did not occur, mainly through ignorance but also because of the unsubtlety of Marxist cultural criticism, which in those days so rarely got down to details, often wasting space by rehearsing, in true religious fashion, the fundamental dogmas of Marxism itself. John Strachey's *The Coming Struggle for Power* exerted, on its publication in 1932, great influence on intellectuals both by putting the Marxist economic and political case with persuasive clarity, and analysing, in equally attractive style, the "decay of capitalist culture", particularly literature. Looking at the latter pages nearly fifty years later, one smiles at their closure to the human spirit's perennial creative capability, their refusal to admit the possibility of the appearance still, under the old order, of an Auden or a *Music of Time*.

As I have said, the iron chain theory of culture had only a short-lived effect on my verse. It was more lasting in such criticism as I wrote (exceedingly sparse, mainly book reviews). My prose fiction was disabled more through lack of maturity and application than ideology. After the war I contemplated casting the loose group into fictive form, may even have written a few pages of a story, but my talent and memory were not up to it. I had kept no journal, so conversations and ideas would have needed re-creation; I felt, too, invented characters would have fallen short of the originals. I think particularly of a waitress called Rose, well into her thirties, if not older; stringy, small, intense; almost always when addressing the group liable to make a fool of herself through losing her thread or through emotion or both — to me embarrassing rather than comic, probably so to all. It comes to me now, remembering her features and black hair, that she may have been Jewish; certainly she was tenaciously left-wing, I think lefter than CPGB, perhaps Trotskyist, a Rosa Luxembourg of the Blackpool cafés. Poor, dear Rose — poor, dear so many of them, selfless in their passion to ameliorate mankind; the noblest of them Maurice Stott, a gentle, stoutish young man, CP member, in comfortable petty bourgeois circumstances, who volunteered for the International Brigade and was swiftly thereafter killed in Spain.

The CP approved (or did not disapprove) of the loose group in Blackpool's peculiar circumstances — industry thin on the ground, seasonal employment, the widespread conservatism of those in the holiday trade and also among the retired come to end their days by the sea. The group was certainly an arena for Marxist proselytization (and as it grew there were increasing candidates for that purpose), but really it was more an enjoyable indulgence than a serious political activity, unless, like John and Sammy, you believed in the necessarily slow capture of sufficient of men's minds by Marxist truth. Rather significant that Marston was an effective performer, inheriting his father's talent for oratory (which I never witnessed publicly displayed, however). Some speaker appeared to present the theories of Major Douglas — economic notions dear to the heart of Ezra Pound. Marston waited till the fools and bores had had their say, then made a brief, annihilating speech, ending with: "What we want is not Social Credit but social revolution." I am sure Marston would have been effective under a revolutionary régime; in the early stages, at any rate. Far from being put to any such test, as he might then have imagined to be on the cards, by staying in Blackpool he prospered in the Councillor's capitalist enterprise.

Even judged from the SPGB standpoint, the loose group undoubtedly became too loose — and transformed into an end in itself — the process, as I heard, even accelerating after I had left the town. Fellows, sockless, wearing sandals, appeared at its meetings, and other crankish types so detested by the pre-war Orwell (not that one holds any brief for Orwell's views in those or, for that matter, any other days). As often happens in such situations, too few of the working-class were involved.

I do not recall Waller ever turning up at the loose group. In any case, his appearances in Blackpool at that epoch were relatively fleeting. I would have said I was still an articled clerk when during the course of a week or so he took me on several visits to a sideshow on Central Promenade. This stretch, between Central Station and Central Pier (where, as related in *Souvenirs*, I had met the writer John Davenport, future collaborator with Dylan Thomas) was — is — known as the Golden Mile because of its favoured position for extracting cash from holiday-makers. Waller had become acquainted with Harold Davidson, ex-Rector of Stiffkey, who at that time was showing himself to the public in a barrel on the Golden Mile. For some now, perhaps then, obscure reason, barrels were fashionable for exhibition purposes, one having been made famous by a man called, or calling himself, Sacco, who offered for a fee to "fast unto death" therein, and I rather think fulfilling his side of the bargain. It may have been the barrel left untenanted by Sacco that came to be occupied by the Reverend Harold Davidson (as he still let himself be known, not accepting his unfrocking for immoral conduct by the Consistory Court, or whatever). An ordinary barrel must not be envisaged: what the filing public saw was a quite commodious affair, with room for a chair and a camp-bed, rather below eye-level. I say "filing public" but there was time and opportunity for the articulate, if they wished, to have a few words with the ex-Rector, the exchange on his side being characteristically fluent, of the hearty, "modern" padre kind, then not so common as it became, though physically he was far from hearty, being thin, slight, nervy, on the border of old age. Since I wrote the foregoing paragraph *The*

Letters of Evelyn Waugh have been published, from which I see that in the summer of 1935 Waugh missed viewing the ex-Rector "by two days". Though the exhibition may have been on in previous summers, it seems more likely that my encounter took place in the days described in the next chapter, rather than those of my articled clerkship. Waugh had been staying with Violet Clifton (mother of the dedicatee of Yeats's "Lapis Lazuli") at Lytham Hall; visited Blackpool one evening, describing it as a "good place". But then he hadn't to live there.

It must have been that Waller had some journalistic project in mind vis-à-vis the ex-Rector, who still proclaimed his innocence when questioned by his customers. I cannot recall anything Waller got out of him in our private conversations. I was struck by the fact that his hair was dyed, and that he was wearing brown make-up which had come off on the inside of his clerical collar, just as such make-up was to be seen discolouring the white ruffs of the pierrot troupe in Happy Valley years before. He had the self-awareness, gave the sense of permanent performance and of a life lived quite far from reality, of one who had been for some time in the public eye, like the politicians and other "celebrities" I met in fair numbers in later years as a Governor of the BBC.

Consequentially enough, in the same sideshow were to be seen living tableaux or artistic poses or however described, though these did not take place in the, or a, barrel, but on a tiny velvet-hung stage in a small room, and a separate entrance fee had to be paid. The sole cast was a quite pretty girl called Eve, no doubt a stage-name, though I may be confusing the name with the title of one of her tableaux. These were announced by the fellow who drew the proscenium curtains back and forth. The pictures briefly revealed were decorously erotic, Eve wearing what today would be called a body-stocking as well as holding fruit, flowers and the like, as relevant and strategically apposite. The white, tight, over-all garment, one realises now, must have been available from theatrical costumiers, had probably been in supply since the days of Adah Isaacs Menken, perhaps before. (Indeed, not long after writing this I came across the word for the thing — "fleshings" — in George R. Sims's *My Life*, in connection with Adah Menken; and I see the OED gives the earliest use of the word as 1838). Needless to say, Waller had also got to know Eve and we had private converse with her, too, a dressing-gown further concealing her charms, as the presenter of the entertainment might have described her anatomy.

She was a nice girl, and I think Waller took her out a couple of times, though I guess what he most enjoyed was demonstrating to me his entrée to this esoteric department of show-biz.

The sideshow episode was typically Wallerian: a wonder it did not somehow come to involve ourselves appearing in a barrel. But it also reveals an ambience that, though in Waller's absence one was not an active part of, nevertheless became more and more uncongenial as boyhood was left behind. The incomprehensions and awakenings of early childhood perhaps made my Oldham years seem in retrospect richer than they were in fact, yet without the least hindsight some Blackpool scenes and society were just about as unrewarding as could be for one who yearned to write well, and for mankind to live well.

5 Unemployed

We know the terrifying brink
From which in dreams you nightly shrink.
"I shall be sacked without," you think,
"A testimonial."

— W. H. Auden

Like the striking girl I eventually sat next to as a common occurrence at the Marston bridge-table, Mrs Spence-Ormerod was a Blackpool figure who eventually became, if not everyday, less than legendary. The name was euphonious (as, in other contexts, Seymour Mead's and Corny Kershaw, mentioned in *Souvenirs*) but the hyphen added a good deal more, to say nothing of its possessor's fashionable, exceedingly stately appearance. I was impressed when my mother got to know her, probably through their both drinking coffee in the mornings in Booth's Café, a large establishment providing good fare, situate above Booth's, a high-class and equally large grocer's.

It could be said that a somewhat classier clientèle was to be found in the café for morning coffee than for afternoon tea, for the latter merged into high tea of plaice and chips substantiality, which one could not imagine Mrs Spence-Ormerod being surrounded by, let alone partaking of. For two of our dwelling-places, the private hotel *Seacliffe* and the flat overlooking the Hotel Metropole, Booth's Café was absurdly convenient, in the same block as the flat, between the Metropole and the North Pier. It had pretensions to fashionableness as well as respectability, and at coffee time, particularly in the holiday season, it was a place where one might expect to see Greeks. This was a term applied by us to anyone of outré looks or dress, through my brother as a young boy once mishearing my mother referring to a group of such figures as "freaks" — the word a typical expression of my mother's detestation of the unconventional.

A decade or so later than my mother's initial acquaintance with Mrs Spence-Ormerod, Booth's Café again came into my life, for my wife and small son, during their wartime exile in Blackpool, sometimes went there to take coffee with my mother, as did I when on leave. Mrs Spence-Ormerod was still an habitué, and the two epochs of my (very slight) knowledge of her have coalesced in my mind, rather like my two visits to Gibson and Weldon. But it was my infant son and not my brother, my wife assures me, who once when addressed by Mrs Spence-Ormerod told her in plain terms to vamoose — highly uncharacteristic, for even at that age he was agreeable, stoical and beautifully behaved. Possibly he was over-reacting to a residual awe inherited from his father. On the other hand, it was surely my brother who in *his* youth referred to her as Mrs Spenc*er*-Ormerod (a usage we privately retained), somewhat augmenting the euphoniousness already noted. One might speculate now that my brother knew perfectly well that the name preceding the hyphen was in fact "Spence" but that the possessor's style and appearance required the normally mute "e" to be pronounced, as in French *chanson* or opera — whether to lend exoticism or bring out the full flavour of "Ormerod" being hazardings perhaps too remote to be sensible.

Mrs Spence-Ormerod had a boy-friend (let the inappropriate nomenclature stand) of a distinction equalling, if not exceeding, her own: Colonel Harold Parker, DSO, a solicitor and County Coroner, often reported in the local press adjudicating on the drowned, etc. He was in practice with his brother in nearby Preston, but they had a branch office in Blackpool — the south end of the town, between Seafolde House and the semi-bungalow of Mrs Sidey where we once had "rooms". A vacancy arose to manage this office, and my mother must simultaneously have been talking about my future with Mrs Spence-Ormerod in Booth's: after an interview with Colonel Parker's brother (far less imposing than his sibling) I was appointed to the post.

Why being a salaried solicitor at one end of the town should be more attractive than at the other I cannot now give reasons for. As soon as I had qualified, Wylie Kay's started paying me £3 a week. It was *ex gratia*, for until my articles expired I had no salary entitlement. With Parker and Parker I was paid £4. 10s a week, but surely I could have jacked Wylie Kay's up to that figure in due course. Or perhaps not. I was keen to get married, so a salary that brought that state closer would have made the new job less like a mere exchange of provincial servitudes than in retrospect it seems.

The Parker and Parker branch consisted of two rooms over a bank, with a staff of one stenographer-office-boy, and a meagre practice. Possibly my predecessor had taken some clients with him. The room I sat in was inappropriately large — the building being of late-Victorian amplitude. The boy was quite good but under-worked: when things were slow I feebly let him go home early. Such business as there was benefited me, at least: I had to do myself what would have been done at Wylie Kay's by minions such as Docking or the cashier or even lesser fry; for instance, issuing a County Court summons, stamping a conveyance. And I had to appear in court under my own steam. In my last days at Wylie Kay's I had done this in the County Court, but only in undefended debt cases before the Registrar, and then my hand was held by the experienced Docking. The fundamentally nervous can never bring themselves to realise that they, too, will in the end master the mechanics of life, however initially strange or enigmatic. Only the other week I came back home with a broken finger-nail, having unconsciously attacked demonically an unfamiliar system of self-service petrol.

I learnt a bit at Parker and Parker: nevertheless was not in the least successful. Hard to say whether at the time I admitted this to myself: certainly I took no steps to change my job, though it is true there proved not to be much time for this. I did not feel hugely ambitious as a solicitor, though not averse to "getting on"; aware that a certain quickness of brain and restless energy distinguished me from the ruck. I would have worked at Parker and Parker's had there been work to do: as it was, the days held time for studying racing form and playing bridge had there been others to share such occupations, as at Wylie Kay's. Whether I wrote verse there, pulling an abstract of title or Inland Revenue Affidavit over the lines if the clerk came in, I fail to recall. But it has just occurred to me that in the summer or autumn of 1934, part of the Parker and Parker epoch, I must have written one of my first published poems, a short piece that appeared in Geoffrey Grigson's *New Verse* in December 1934. (The emotion felt receiving a copy of the magazine with the breakfast post in the house overlooking Stanley Park is recapturable still.) It was a freakish turn-up for the sort of poem that might be classed as just passable for its time (*New Verse* did not take another poem of mine for more than a year), not reprinted until James Gibson, in the early Seventies, asked me to contribute to his enterprising book *Let the Poet Choose* (an anthology made by the contributing poets themselves), where in my note to the poem I said that "For an unknown provincial young man, to achieve publication in a first-class avant-garde magazine . . . came as an excitement and encouragement scarcely to be experienced again." The poem begins:

> In a normal rainfall the channel was adequate,
> but all that summer under dripping trees,
> I waited watching pyrotechnics on macadam.

The absence of political moralising and the presence of comparative concreteness is notable compared with my other verse of the time. Why didn't I see the advantage in this? The poem goes on to tell of the disasters of excessive rainfall. One is reminded of the rather well-worn story of John Piper's water-colours of Windsor Castle, done with his usual dramatic cloudy skies and lurid light. George VI, looking through them, having given permission for the artist to be there — perhaps commissioned him — remarked: "Pity about the weather."

Further as to success in the law: in a few years time, after Parker and Parker, I was on the way to modest achievement. The process continued after the War. Yet I felt comparatively unmoved about the thing until at the age of forty-six, as well as being solicitor to the Woolwich Building Society, I became legal advisor to the Building Societies Association, and a little later on sat on a Law Society committee working on conveyancing law reform. Perhaps such activities revived my old taste for action: quite suddenly I was able to influence legislation, pull the legs of quite distinguished colleagues; in Reithian terms, be more "stretched". I enjoyed it, but was rescued, if that is the word, from its constricting more and more the literary side of things, by being given the opportunity to retire prematurely from the law, which I did.

How far such a future from the solitary and rather run-down office above the Bank! A few existing and loyal clients came in, and I may have introduced one or two new ones, at best family friends with wills to make, in those days a simple and cheap job. I don't recall doing any work for the comrades, in any case mostly propertyless by definition — and if Sammy ever had problems over foreign bodies found in meat pies, and the like, he did not consult me. What a contrast, forty-five years later, when many radical solicitors make a very decent living through subsidised barrack-room lawyerdom!

The bulk of the callers at Parker and Parker's Blackpool branch wanted to take, not confer, business — insurance inspectors, stationery salesmen, *et al.* Some semi-scroungers also appeared, as in a comedy by Ben Jonson, the word presumably having got round that a new green manager was to be found at the top of the stairs beside the Bank. The most persistent of these was a small crippled man who had, or said he had, invented a hospital bed, and was looking for capital to manufacture or otherwise exploit it. Eventually he prevailed on me to visit his house, where a prototype of the bed was to be seen. I expect he realised I would never provide any trusting clients with cash to spare, but he probably saw in myself a source of funds. With his rubber-tipped stick he pointed out the bed's novel features, chief of which was a facility for tilting head and foot separately, appropriate to the patient's needs. It was an iron bedstead, painted white; the colour lending authenticity. Whether the bed was really a prototype, the winding mechanism novel, I do not know. No money was extracted from me; not that I had any to extract. A good bit afterwards I read a newspaper paragraph about the conviction of the inventor for fraud involving the bed, but this may not necessarily have extended to the originality of the device. I used the figure of the cripple in a short story published in *Folios of New Writing* in 1941; and the atmosphere of the affair was somehow revived when, much later, I read the pages about Peter Doyle in Nathanael West's *Miss Lonelyhearts*. Why certain episodes in life of apparent triviality make such an effect, particularly vis-à-vis creativity, is somewhat mysterious; though in this case my taste for the grotesque and the criminal was clearly being appealed to. I ought to add, what now forcibly strikes me, that my four-year-old son for some time amiably mocked me by calling me "Roy Fuller the pig." The title of the story ("The Pig") appeared in *Folios of New Writing* below my name, set without punctuation. His humorous precocity was also illustrated when, on the coming into being a few years later of John Lehmann's *New Writing and Daylight*, he a trifle cruelly referred to it as *Old Writing and Moonlight*.

When, after Parker and Parker days, I was applying for jobs, I was able to put a plausible gloss of success on my managership of the branch by prefacing mention of it with the strictly accurate rubric "1934–35", as though it were a rung in my career, but I doubt if the experience lasted a full twelve months. Not long after I arrived, Arthur Parker suddenly died, and not long after that his brother merged his practice with that of a firm that had a branch in Preston and its main office in Blackpool. The Preston office of W. and B. Blackhurst was to be closed; likewise the Blackpool office of Parker and Parker. It may well have been that the latter action had not been finally decided upon before a visit one day by Colonel Parker and the two Blackhursts to the offices above the Bank.

Colonel Parker had been a Territorial, perhaps still was: with his clipped grey moustache and soldierly bearing could have come from the pages of Agatha Christie, the friendship with Mrs Spence-Ormerod (also an Agathaean name and character) affording the necessary tinge of suspicion (though to have the Coroner himself guilty would have been quite a supreme stroke, even for that author). I knew the Blackhursts, by sight at least. William was a dark, stout, forceful man in his forties, well known in the Courts; his brother much milder, on the conveyancing side. I don't suppose I relished this encounter in the least: indeed, my inability to recapture now its feeling-tone may imply chagrin, even shame. The fact was the office just about failed to break even (as I well knew, having had to learn to keep the books as well as grapple with the clerks, sometimes of Kafkaesque superciliousness, at the County Court offices). "How would you set about building up the practice?" W. Blackhurst asked me. I said something about joining a golf club, what I imagined to be received wisdom. Had I specified the Masons it would have been no farther from my inclinations or intentions. Though W. Blackhurst refrained from enquiring why then I remained a non-golfer, I realised only too well how little he must have been impressed with that and my other observations. He was precisely the type of human to succeed in those departments of life where I would be found to be most lacking, and I expect I was not much surprised that the closure of the branch was unaccompanied by the offer of a post in the main Blackpool office. The further irony probably failed to occur to me that a social life that included membership of the Loose Group was fundamentally a negative asset in the career of a solicitor of those days, though had W. Blackhurst been aware of it he might have thought it some evidence of character at least in one, from his viewpoint, so apparently feeble.

So in 1935 I was unemployed, could rightfully have joined a procession of the kind organized by the National Unemployed

Workers Movement that I had watched with compassion a few years before from the articled clerks' room at Wylie Kay's. It was hard to get another job. My application letters necessarily revealed a brief and quite commonplace start to a career; and when called to an interview I see now I was far too self-denigratory about lack of experience. Such kind of honesty is no doubt a species of self-regard, but it did me no good at the time, unless preserving me for an appointment that proved to suit me as well as anything could by way of legal destiny. I had some near misses. For an assistant solicitorship in the West End I went for an interview to the principal's house in Ealing, he being indisposed — though I began to doubt this when he kept introducing the topic of corporal punishment into the conversation, a form of advance I was by then able to recognize and more or less adroitly parry. Should I have taken the post, if offered, and like the narrator in Proust moved unperverted into a perverted world? After the war I used to see the solicitor's letter-heads among the vast legal correspondence coming into the Woolwich Equitable solicitor's department: the principal had by then acquired a few junior partners; whether he kept them in order by strict means I used to wonder. At an interview in the legal department of the Post Office I harped on my lack of practice in registered conveyancing (as though that demanded years of study and practice). What a nit-wit! The appointment would have brought me to London and into an organization where I could have scarcely failed to get on.

Another job I applied for was as assistant solicitor with the Manchester firm of T. A. Higson and Co. That may not have been the precise firm name, though T. A. Higson was senior partner, or within a whisker of it. Being interviewed is part of the mistier recesses of memory, though it comes to me that T. A. Higson himself looked in on the proceedings, even if not himself conducting them. I believe I worsened my chances of getting the job by being too shy to make a few acute observations about McDonald's bowling action or the like, for though I knew that as well as being a solicitor of eminence, Higson was chairman of the committee of the Lancashire County Cricket Club, I never ingratiated myself with him by indicating my own interest in the game.

Quite soon I was prepared to go anywhere, certainly to continue in Blackpool where, in fact, an opportunity or two arose, including a partnership with a youngish solicitor who not much later went to prison for fraudulent conversion. The Parcae, though shilly-shallying about me in this area, were favourable on the whole. When it became clear I wasn't going to walk into a job I ordered a sign and had it affixed to one of the garden gate posts of the house (the house we had moved to after leaving the house overlooking Stanley Park, the latter being found by my mother, in one of her troughs of health, too large to be easily managed):

R. B. FULLER
SOLICITOR

Strangely enough, a little higher up, across the road, was the house occupied by Mrs Spence-Ormerod. Did Colonel Parker, on his visits, guiltily observe this feeble evidence of his former employee's struggle to re-establish himself in the law? Our house was miles away from the town's commercial hub, though quite near the North Shore Golf Club, which the Colonel may have imagined I had belatedly joined.

A few passers-by were actually enticed in by the sign, not of the Peter Doyle variety but neither of the substance to enable me to make a living. I wonder now quite how I passed the abundant time available. There were Party activities and the Loose Group. I liked watching football and cricket, as has been seen. I was a member of Boots' Booklovers Library (a great boon of those days and after) as well as of the Public Library: my reading was non-stop but desultory. My wife-to-be and I had friends in addition to those already touched on. There was the Metropole pianist and his wife, mentioned in *Souvenirs*; and the organist whose acceptable wedding-present was to play at our wedding, held in church not only to prevent my mother's grief but also to please my wife's parents. He duly married his fiancée of those days, also a friend, but later divorced her, whereupon she married Marston, whose first wife, introduced to him in London by Waller and known to me on my London sojourns, was by then dead. Since I greatly admired books like *The Old Wives' Tale*, I suppose I saw, even before reading Proust, that a vast area of fictional interest lay in the amatory gyrations among small groups in society, time and propinquity bringing about the unlikeliest permutations and combinations. But I would never have thought to treat such matters in my fiction, even had I found power to do so. The minutiae of life, often of what I have called the nose-picking variety, and later crime, absorbed me. For as well as writing verse, I continued to make attempts at prose fiction, ambition of my schooldays. But at prose as well as verse I always worked as

Dr Kettle (reported by Aubrey) said Seneca wrote — "as a Boare doth pisse, *scilicet* by jirkes."

Would a surviving father, an earlier epoch, or a higher education have to some extent counteracted this appalling absence of discipline? No doubt I felt my life had purpose, particularly in the direction of being in love and wanting to settle down, but a good few of its aims spattered or missed the target. I think I am being honest in this description of my literary ability, yet I would not be telling the whole story if I did not add that even today, comparing it with genius, or mere talent of others, I may try to make out of its deficiencies a virtue that I tell myself indubitably great and industrious writers lack — to their disadvantage. It is the crudest and most illogical kind of self-esteem: for instance, after having just read Evelyn Waugh's war-time letters to his wife I try to think of some advantage mine have over his though there is not the shadow of a doubt his are abundantly worthwhile and mine not worth an outsider reading.

6 A Phantom Voice

thou spok'st of Pogromites, of the Vapians passing the
equinoctial of Querbus.

— Twelfth Night

Though perhaps sufficiently confusing the reader, I have not here, nor in *Souvenirs*, listed exhaustively the various houses, flats and furnished rooms we occupied between my father's death and my marriage. One move was caused by the emotional failure of a return to Oldham, not long after the former event; another arose because we failed successfully to share a house with friends — an episode I'm sure full of comedy, even farce, but largely lost to my memory no doubt on account of my being the main dissentient, an early display of testiness about such things, unimportant to some, as the brewing and serving of a breakfast beverage. All the other changes, however, were prompted by the ups and downs of my mother's health.

Since Sir William Jenner was not impossibly tardy in 1871 in recognizing the symptoms of Graves' Disease in Christina Rossetti, it seems astonishing that in the Thirties my mother went undiagnosed for so long. Indeed, one piece of advice she received savoured very much of the faith-healing side of Victorian medicine: she was told she ought to take a prolonged sea voyage. I am not sure if the doctor himself did not suggest a practical and reasonably inexpensive way of doing this, viz. to buy a season ticket for the steamers that plied between Fleetwood, a little way up the Fylde coast, and Douglas in the Isle of Man. Anyway, this is what my mother did, making the trip perhaps two or three times a week, sometimes having to endure boisterous weather, I think seldom if ever disembarking, simply waiting for the boat to back out from the quay at Douglas — an episode in her life like a story by Kafka, or, perhaps more accurately, that play by Sutton Vane where the characters are mysteriously condemned to shipboard life, without possibility (in most cases) of return — a play that as will be seen later had its application to my own experiences. Inevitably she came to know other season ticket holders, who were mostly dedicated boozers, for the ship's bars opened as soon as the vessel cast off, whatever the time of day. An entirely sober couple, however, who I believe took to sea simply to fill in an otherwise rather empty turn to their lives, became particular friends, the relationship continuing when sailing days were done.

Mr and Mrs Parslew were in latish middle-age. He had made his modest pile, was virtually retired, though retaining some undemanding business interest, probaly a non-executive directorship. His personality was dominating, not to say domineering; geniality sometimes showing an edge of irascibility undoubtedly alarming to anyone dependent on his money, or obliged by ties of duty or blood to stick with him, or even to friends and acquaintances of mild temperament. His face and bald head (the latter fringed by cropped grey hair) were beaten by the weather of the Irish Sea; later, when, like Ulysses, he had given up his voyagings, the effect was sustained by the sun striking through the sliding roof of his Armstrong Siddeley motor car, quite a novel feature in those days, as was the car's pre-selective gears, with lever on the steering-wheel. He said more than once he had lost his hair in early youth through washing it in ammonia, the motive for this drastic absterging never being made utterly clear, though the action very much in character. The toilet fluid he preferred when we knew him was "Larola", a complexion milk. The label on the bottle depicted the head of a girl with wind-swept hair, rather old-fashioned, the use of the preparation being indicated by a phrase in inverted commas, as though a quotation from a poem, which it may have been — "In summer's heat and winter's cold." The Isle of Man steamers and the Armstrong Siddeley roof had given Larola a good testing, and it scarcely needed the urging of Mr Parslew (always ready to commend his own habits) for me to use it myself. Moreover, there was always the chance it would do my pimples good: hope unfulfilled.

Mrs Parslew, stouter than her husband, was placid and uncomplaining, though had a good deal to put up with. Should she be injudicious enough to yawn during the evening, and be spotted by her husband, he would say Quilpishly: "You're tired, Mother. Go to bed." If the hour were not ridiculously early she might well depart; hardship alleviated by her taking "supper" with her, always in the form of cheese. My mother used to report her eating as much as half a pound on such occasions, but as I have said elsewhere my mother laid it on thick about traits she considered eccentric. Some nocturnal trouble of Mrs Parslew's was ascribed by my mother to this caseous habit — not nightmare, that would have been too obvious; possibly snoring. Another confidence imparted to us by Mr Parslew was that what had originally attracted him to Mrs Parslew, impelled him to marry her, was her ugliness. It should be said that the cognomen "Mother", used by Mr Parslew, resulted from their having a nubile daughter, who frequently sang to herself a popular song of the day:

> I'm on a see-saw.
> You throw me up and you throw me down,
> I don't know whether I'm here or there.

Why my brother should find this funny, and make me laugh about it, too, is now unclear.

Mr Parslew's energy was excessive for the occupations of retirement. "Get on the job right away" was an admonition he urged on others as well as himself. Deciding on even a modest trip required him to resolve to have the Armstrong Siddeley "oiled and greased" forthwith. These two phrases my brother and I began to use interchangeably to express an intention to act, getting "oiled and greased" being applied by us to the human preliminaries. I have no doubt Mr Parslew had observations to make about my joblessness; probably commanded that I put that sign on the gatepost. He specified £1000 a year as an indication of success in life: no further comment from him was needed to bring home to me how far I was from that goal, even before I was unemployed.

He actually determined the general future of my brother's life. My mother's sailings to Douglas was merely a further strand in the ties we already had with the Isle of Man, as specified in *Souvenirs* (and which I was tickled to see added to by Frank Kermode, a Manxman, actually reviewing that book). But by then my brother must have left King William's College, was probably an usher (as he derogatorily called himself) at a prep school in St Annes-on-the-Sea where, though his academic qualifications were meagre, he

73

filled an apparently long-felt want as a fourth at bridge with the headmaster and his wife, and the matron. Still, that was too slender a foundation for a career. As well as qualifications, my brother lacked ideas about how to earn a living. He was extremely fond of reading, wrote a bit, was handsome and dressed well. Perhaps he should have followed up his early success as the Apothecary, and gone on the stage.

Mr Parslew was convinced that the hotel world offered a future for the smart, decently educated young person of respectable family (that such a notion, as novel then as the pre-selective gear, is now a commonplace is due to a considerable extent to my brother's work in the field of hotel and catering education). It may be Mr Parslew had contacts in that world. Certainly my brother was quite expeditiously oiled and greased and interviewed in London by one of the Salmons, the family that ran Joe Lyons, who accepted him as an apprentice. Soon after, he was sweating in the kitchens of the Regent Palace Hotel, getting up at four to go to Smithfield with the meat-buyer for Lyons' London hotels; the shabby but leisurely gentility of the usher's life vanished. Perhaps any resistence to this arduous and unknown world had been undermined by his admiration for Arnold Bennett's novel about a hotel, *Imperial Palace*, then not long published.

It occurs to me not to leave too depressed an impression of my workless days.

> Your pockets gape with wry dismay,
> Turned inside-out we find them funny:
> Strange, now I cannot laugh again
> For fear my tears should fall like rain.

— Stephen Spender's poem (subsequently rather spoiled by being made less specific, as explained later) addressed to a member of the unemployed, familiar from *Oxford Poetry 1930*, was not at all apropos. I think my mother gave me ten shillings a week. There would be a few meagre fees from my few clients. Out of her wages my wife-to-be paid her whack. We continued with our entertainments, modest, but that nevertheless might put us cheek by jowl with Blackpool's élite — in seats booked for the Sunday evening showing of the film *Queen Christina*, say, or for a concert by Duke Ellington and his band. In a sense, and even in actuality, we knew some of the promoters of the annual Spinsters' Ball, of the members of the North Shore Golf Club; though our social life was passed with the Loose Group and its denizens.

It must have been the late winter of 1935–36 that in answer to my application I was asked to go — what seemed a really immense trek — to Ashford in Kent to be interviewed for an assistant solicitorship with a firm called Kingsford, Flower and Pain. By that time I had devised what now seems a very ordinary, not to say egregious formula, but which I then considered fresh and keen-seeming, for the start of my application letters: "I am extremely interested in your advertisement" etc. I do believe this plunging more or less *in medias res* may have secured more response than my near-minimal experience and qualifications warranted. Another phrase used, picked up from somewhere or another, and striking me as a modest way of commending in advance my looks and turn-out, was: "I am of good appearance and address." I see now that both these ploys may have specially appealed to Frank Flower, the senior partner in Kingsford, Flower and Pain. When Jack Clark (of whom more anon) read in *Souvenirs* of Tom Wylie Kay's fourteen guinea Savile Row suits, he told me that Frank Flower patronized the same thoroughfare at the same price. Evidently Frank Flower was not too disillusioned when, following my letter, I appeared for interview in something from the Blackpool tailors, Southworths, for I was taken on.

Probably guilt has caused me to disremember the effect on my mother of the prospect of my leaving her and my brother, presumably for good, but I think she was stoical. In the event my brother never went back to Blackpool to live, either, and she gave up the house, went to live with friends — not the Parslews, that relationship somehow dying away. Mr Parslew may have thought somewhat better of me for quitting the ranks of the unemployed, though still far from his criterion of success in life, my starting salary being £286 a year.

Writing these last few pages, I have been struck by the contrast between them and what has come down the years as the atmosphere and aspirations of the Thirties (I say nothing of the almost unre-capturable density of life — people, objects, sensations, in their actuality, not simply as traditions or half-memories or impossibly difficult exercises in the literary commonplace). One thing there is no need to labour is the despairing sense then possessed of a succession of wrong decisions taken by authority, decisions that could never be remedied, that brought us nearer doom. This period inculcated a pessimism that lasted far beyond the period itself: I recall being amazed, post-war, at the welcome collapse of the Central African Federation, which I imagined would inevitably impose the injustices of what was then Southern Rhodesia on states more appropriately black-ruled (though whether such collapse has in fact added to the sum of African happiness is an elderly buffer's query *ex post facto*). In the Thirties the prime exemplar of gloom was the so-called non-interventionist policy over the Spanish Civil War. At that time, too, the long-feared anticipation of general war bringing with it the aerial bombardment of civilians, was given concrete form.

I think not until well into the Second World War did one lose the sense that one oneself might yet see a social revolution conducted, to a degree at least, in the terms of armed conflict (an English storming of the Winter Palace, as it were) — the old sense, though much modified by the decade's amazing historical tergiversations, of the closeness of great change, ushered in by the events that followed the Wall Street crash. More or less vague anxieties about a possible capitalist war against the Soviet Union — a continuation of the post-1918 war of intervention — had hardened with fascism's taking of power in Germany. The idea that democratic capitalism might, against the odds, almost against its own interests, join with the Soviet Union to oppose the fascist powers, was unsupported by most of the evidence going, and too much of a happy ending to be plausibly historical in apocalyptic days. Moreover, it seemed simply self-deluding to conceive that mere alliance would deter the fascists making war — an ingredient of fascism's role, by definition. And despair about conventional political leaders in the democracies did not wholly stem from Marxist convictions: they seemed, in Auden's phrase, irredeemably "Holders of one position, wrong for years."

The phrase (from the 1930 *Poems*) represents a side of Auden immediately congenial. His influence continued in various ways. I have found and brought down the trunk-in-the-loft poems previously referred to. I had envisaged a ring-file of typescripts, but the object in question proved to be a twelve inch by seven-and-a-half "Memoranda or Minute Book" (as entitled on the stout cover). Surely I must have bought this in imitation of a note-book used by the young Auden, and described as a butcher's ledger, though I can find no reference to that romantically anti-romantic article in either the Auden double number of *New Verse* or *Lions and Shadows*, so the source of my knowledge stays mysterious somewhat. I started in

March 1935 to copy poems into my book, sometimes feebly working on them, up to the autumn of 1937. Not all my output is there, but I guess a substantial tranche of it is. A few more poems unsystematically appear in the book right up into the early months of 1939.

The proletcult poems at the beginning of the notebook are, to adopt Poirot's phrase, "bad, but bad, and of a badness" — versification of the crudest left ideas. Some of the idiocies, like those in Wordsworth and moralistic Victorian verse, may be the result of an intention to write poetry the masses could understand and be influenced by; that could be printed in the *Daily* alongside prose about injustice to seasonal workers. I will not give any specimen of these, for the temptation is too strong to mislead by choosing passages that some fact of the times, or some word-concatenation, has slightly enlivened. The smiling moustaches poem is not complete, but some of it seems to date from early 1936, too late for present comfort. Incidentally, Valentine Cunningham's remarkable *Penguin Book of Spanish Civil War Verse*, published at the time I wrote the foregoing words, confirms how the political poetry of the period could in fact move non-intellectual audiences (though such audiences, it is true, were usually as predominantly left as that which heckled the future Lord Martonmere).

In the autumn of 1935 — with more certainty in the Spring of 1936 — an improvement may be detected in the Minute Book poems, though probably only by those reading with extreme sympathy. Elements of Marxism are replaced to some degree by Gravesian fables; and a few observations of nature appear:

> From what far country blow the winds that rattle
> The old ivy on those trees?

That line and a half dates from my arrival in Ashford; the aural phenomenon (commonplace enough) noted on an early solitary walk. I will let the Shakespearean epigraph stand at the head of this chapter, though looking through my poems of this period I am surprised how transparent they are. I had imagined far more obfuscation and pseudo-reference, particularly in verse rejected by the editors of those days, but there is a fairly uniform mix of naiveté, propaganda, and unprofound poetic "plotting", not at all hard at any point to comprehend, or so it seems to me now. Within the conventions of the period (which dominate in a strange way, not easy to explain, the feebler poets knocking about), Ashford and its environs may be recognized in some of the pieces. In a ballad (not included in the Minute Book, however), the phrase "blunt, proper knives for scraping scab" was derived from the agricultural window of the Ashford "Boots the Chemists", where such implements were displayed for sale, an enterprising side of the chain never before encountered. The epithets were added by me, "proper" being in the neutral mode then rather favoured by poets.

I recognize the origin of another poem in some visits I had to make to a client of Kingsford, Flower and Pain incarcerated in a lunatic asylum. The business made a considerable impression on me. Hard to say whether dottiness was a period obsession or something of more personal interest; though perhaps any form of the irrational has its appeal, even to the most cerebral of poets. At any rate, I was wholly engaged by the madman's youth and the virtual impossibility of communicating with him; by his inimitably mad letters, not least their handwriting and layout; and the bleak austerity and routine of the institution itself. Almost none of this appears in the poem: pretty well everything is elevated, abstract, stiff.

> The insane are not crafty, they are great
> With smiles that turn conventional gestures
> To blows against pathetic power.

Today such a poem (the "confessional" tradition lively), even from a mediocre poet, would be personal and circumstantial — more interesting and less daft, but whether better, in the sense of being at all readable by posterity, than the fifth-rate in the earlier mode, who knows?

I was primarily taken on by Kingsford's to relieve Frank Flower from the burden of going into court. He was weary of the duty; besides, despite having fixed the minimum fee for appearing in the Police Court at three guineas (then a respectable sum, as my starting salary implies), he could occupy his time far more remuneratively. Conveyancing and other non-contentious work would also fall to my lot. On that afternoon of my interview it so happened that Frank Flower had been delayed somewhere away from the office, so I saw the junior partner, Harold E. Pain, and then waited for Frank Flower in the latter's office on the first floor back, a pleasant room (with white-painted shelves holding a good library, including the

Law Reports) though looking out merely at and over commercial Ashford.

I suppose the two partners were much of an age. Harold Pain had been a "ten year man" — serving only three years' articles, having already had ten years in the law as a solicitor's clerk. He was a bachelor, lived with his sister, a spinster: tallish, slim, he turned himself out in a manner that even then seemed old-fashioned. I daresay (typical of my unthoroughness or shyness, I never bothered to enquire — though had I been tactful there might well have been an interesting response) some venerable Ashford tailor made — perhaps had always made — his suits. They were invariably (but can that really have been so?) clerical grey, cut high in the lapel, narrow in the trouser, in a fashion that, after the war, astonishingly made some sort of come-back. His collars were starched, spectacles gold-rimmed, moustache so abundant that when his cigarette had burnt down (he smoked by letting the weed burn between his lips) he had to withdraw it from his mouth by inserting his finger and thumb *below* the grizzled whisker. The hair was slightly grizzled, too, and fine, brushed close to a small, rather elegant head, and finished off with an unexaggerated quiff. (One might also have enquired about his barber). Really the style was not tremendously far from the Van Dyke mode already touched on, another unlikely come-back. Harold Pain's competency as a lawyer was great; his kindness and geniality unvarying — though a tone of sad reproof might briefly come over his voice on his discovery of incompetence, even to the extent of a "tck", approaching actual annoyance. About the ordinary affairs of humanity (moving house, say, or dying) with which his professional work was pretty well exclusively concerned, he spoke with a committed enjoyment almost gastronomic at moments of greatest enthusiasm when one detected a faint slushing of saliva under some of his words — words that seemed to come from an accumulation of speech at the front of his mouth, perhaps impeded in their emergence by the moustache.

He taught me a lot; some I should have already known had I been made to serve my articles more conscientiously. "I am accustomed to working without supervision," I used to write, accurately but rather misleadingly, when applying for jobs, but with Kingsford's much of my work was overseen, certainly at first, mainly by the partners, though also by the extremely efficient conveyancing and litigation managing clerks. Probably from the outset I had given indication of professional deficiencies. I once took to Mr Pain a conveyance I had drafted — of part of Sir Charles Igglesden's ample garden, surplus to requirements, Sir Charles being a local newspaper proprietor, chairman of the Ashford magistrates. I sat at Mr Pain's side while he wrote in, with fluent hand and brain, the grant and reservation of those rights and easements (we were acting for both parties) I had omitted, a fairly elementary but comprehensive lesson in visualising the practical use of property I never forgot — getting down to the classic case of Blackacre and Whiteacre, as it were, instead of being dilettanti about Purpleacre and Puceacre.

Frank Flower was a less patient taskmaster. He had a habit, particularly when standing, of holding a document by the stapled or paper-clipped corner between his right thumb and fore-finger, the document supported for his eye by the right wrist and forearm, turning the sheets back with his left hand. No doubt that was how he viewed a draft lease I once submitted for his approval, though only the perusal of a leaf or two was necessary before he tossed the thing back to me, saying: "That's not a full repairing lease." I was chagrinned as much by his withering tone as by my failure to carry out instructions (perhaps at that date not even grasping the implications of the phrase "full repairing"). I went off burning with a resentment damped down by guilt.

I myself acquired the document-holding trick, found myself still occasionally doing it when I came back into the law after war service. It was not the only habit I copied from Frank Flower. He had a brief loud laugh, throwing back his head to emit it. In moments of concentration he compressed his lips and, since his countenance was florid, I used fancifully to think the tightness of mouth was to prevent an outflow of blood. Why I should imitate these two idiosyncrasies I do not know, though Frank Flower impressed me from the moment he came late into his office where I was waiting — I think passing the time by reading a volume of the Law Reports, always containing something fresh and good — that first afternoon. He was wearing his navy-blue overcoat and bowler-hat (an indication, I came to know later, of some expedition out of the usual), and with his Savile Row suit his invariable bow tie. As to the suit, Jack Clark, after reading *Souvenirs*, told me that Frank Flower, in the days I am writing of, once said to him: "Feel that, my lad," putting Jack's fingers on the coat of his suit, and adding with only superficial inconsequence: "Who gets the furcoats in Russia, the *moujiks* or Mrs Stalin?"

I inherited from Frank Flower, too, to a degree, an emphatic, articulated way of speaking; though this may have resulted any way from my initial endeavour to bring my style of speech up to educated southern standards, for friends made in Ashford brought home to me that the injunctions from the Boss at school as to not mumbling, to say nothing of correct "u" and "a" sounds, and the hard and soft "g", had in my case been incompletely mastered. I suppose it must be admitted that the fundamental motive for altering one's accent is snobbish, yet self-improvement in other spheres is considered worthy. What I evolved, as heard by me in B.B.C. recordings and the like, was a neutral, quite passable and I believe not bogus mode, which often inclined (as did my grandfather's speech in olden days) to the more demotic within the family or on encountering some friend whose origins had been in the north, such as Richard Hoggart or Anthony Thwaite. A strange thing is — and the penny didn't drop about this until late in life — that I am sure the accent I converted over the years was more Yorkshire than Lancashire. Though I have gone through life reckoning myself a Professor Higgins in identifying Lancashire and Yorkshire accents, in fact in true Thirties fashion I was a frontier figure myself, I'm sure never possessing the soft tones and exaggerated "r" rounds of typical industrial Lancashire (in an Oldham programme on the radio not long ago I noticed "purr-ents" ("parents"), taking me back, but not to my own habits), let alone the esoteric tones of more rural districts, as exemplified in the speech of George Woodcock, say, the trade unionist. When I fall into proletarian speech, I believe it has a Yorkshire tincture — perhaps now influenced by Northern comedians rather than the natural ways of my boyhood. On the other hand, I may be underestimating how far the East Lancashire accent familiar in early boyhood was overlaid in memory and familiarity by that of the Fylde coast. Norman Lees, the engrossing clerk at Wylie Kay's, sometimes used to quote two lines of verse in the mode in which (he said) they were recited at his secondary school:

> 'Is breast was burr, 'is matted 'urr
> Was burried in the sand . . .

Donkey's years later I was astounded to encounter these lines, so familiar in garbled form, in the first stanza of Longfellow's utterly serious poem, "The Slave's Dream".

To go back to Frank Flower, whatever he came to think of my legal ability, it strikes me now that the initial favourable impression was mutual, because though he asked Mr Pain to come into his room before the decision was actually made, it was he who engaged me. Kingsford's occupied the middle position of the three substantial firms in the town (there was a one-man band that scarcely counted). Below it was a firm also with a title in the metre of Matthew Arnold's "elegiacs": Poncia, Swann and Carter — though I think Arnold would not have admitted the feminine ending. Poncia, like Kingsford, was dead: his lingering name, suggestive of the Mafia, or Maltese undesirables, lent the firm a faintly sinister air, to some extent borne out by Swann, Carter and the managing clerk all having crooked noses. The fault was a common one in that the nose did not grow straight out of the face, though the side to which it inclined differed in two of the cases, I forget which; but that is scarcely of importance. I think it was Mervyn Bompas, a junior partner in Hallett, Creery and Co., who drew my attention to the phenomenon.

Hallett, Creery and Co., the town's premier firm, spoilt the metre by eventually shortening themselves to Hallett and Co. Hallett and Creery were both goners, and such was the size, class and prestige of the firm there had been no need to promote even the most senior on the quite long list of partners to the firm name. Last on the list was Mervyn, fairly recently recruited. I first ran across him in the Ashford County Court, where he was welcoming and agreeable; made the first move towards meeting non-professionally. He was blond, broad, not tall; open countenance, small nose; scion of a legal family — I think it was his great-grandfather who had been Dickens's model for Sergeant Buzfuz. Now, I find it hard to think myself back to a time when his life-style — that of the professional middle-class, untinged by Blackpool's vulgarities — seemed, if not alien, at least possible in some of its turns to catch one embarrassingly out. I am putting the business in too favourable a light: I expect I made as many unconscious boobs in behaviour as I tried to avoid or cover up.

From Mervyn, always correct but quite without side, I quickly learnt a bit of *comme il faut*. Soon after I arrived in Ashford he moved out of digs into a flat, where his way of life was less tramelled. A half-loaf of bread, brown and not pristine, on a bread-board on the luncheon table, with a bread-knife to help oneself, was far from what my mother or grandmother would have thought proper or even edible. Yet I recognized in the careless austerity — as in the flat's sparse furniture and occasional *objet* — a positive good, as might reside in the Spartan lavatorial facilities of some establishment of great learning. Mervyn drove me one Sunday to London to visit his mother and step-father. They lived in a flat in the region of Westminster Cathedral, the sort of place where the Widmerpools and Leonard Short were to live. Proper (the scab-knife epithet comes readily to the pen) cultivated trappings were there even more in evidence; the mother good-looking, intelligent, sharp; the step-father big, elderly, maybe to be addressed as "Colonel", I am not sure.

We were friends with Mervyn all through our Ashford days: his influence continued. He conferred on my wife the shortened name "Kate", still used; had a habit of standing after a meal, to let (as he said) gravity aid digestion — still referred to. What he made of my political views I do not recall, if I ever knew.

I suppose Kate and I would have married on any salary paid by a job of prospective permanency, adjusting life-style to cash available. Flats to rent were available in Ashford, even at our notional maximum mark of twenty-five shillings a week — though at such a price always possessing some bizarre feature, like the bath (covered with a bath-shaped board) being in the kitchen, or (in the case of a flat over a warehouse) the sitting-room being of grotesque amplitude. We settled on one in a village called Kennington (now virtually a suburb) two or three miles outside the town, above a sweet-shop, on offer at seventeen shillings and sixpence a week, rates inclusive. The bizarre feature here was the kitchen, so tiny it seemed doubtful whether there would be room for more than one person to stand in it when a cooker had been installed. A good job my mother saw the premises only as a *fait accompli*. By relinquishing their offer to redecorate the interior, I beat the landlords down to sixteen shillings.

Thus two townees came to live, if not quite in the country, as close to it as they ever would. Did I try to observe and learn about natural phenomena, as I would, however feebly, today? The answer cannot be deduced from my verse of the time. We were not far from Eastwell Park, a beauteous estate then owned by Viscount Dunsford, and once the home of the excellent early eighteenth century poet Anne Finch, Countess of Winchilsea. One could walk through the park, past the great house, to the little church, where there was an elaborate monument to the Countess. It seems I was less interested as a poet in landscape and wild creatures than a literary and anachronistic version of aristocratic life — weak heirs, mouldering peers' robes, and so forth:

Inside the topmost room
The wellfed spectre
The corpulent ancestor
The vampire sector.

We knew a good few residents of Kennington, particularly after
our son's birth, when his pram was benignly overlooked by the
elderly and offered to be pushed by admiring schoolgirls. Though
we anatomized their peculiarities (and our own, such as Kate's
asking in vain for donkey-stone at the village general shop, wanting
in her early enthusiasm to tart-up the step leading to the sixteen-
shilling flat), I think I never regarded the place in imaginative
terms, even as the hierarchical setting for a whodunnit. I see now
how lightly I took the prospect of being both a writer and a lawyer,
letting the former occupation almost take care of itself, relying on
the arrival of inspiration, such as it was. It could be argued that
this was so until fairly recent times, when, my lawyering days over,
time could scarcely be passed without some slightly more systematic
ordering of literary activity.

When I began to publish poetry and fiction regularly after the
war, surprise expressed at this accompanying a nine to five job did
nothing to remove a sense of guilt about my indolence. I expect
some people thought my grandfather's life (Superintendent Registrar, Alderman, Magistrate) one of dutiful assiduity, but I felt
myself growing more and more like him, success merely some
unwilled trick; the double man, indeed, being just as interested, if
not more so, in a third existence — in my grandfather's case, playing
bridge, buying prize cheese, and such domestic eccentricities as
playing "golf" (cherished trivialities paralleled in my own life).

Knowing one Kennington family, the Clarks, had long perspectives. They lived, as we did, on the main Ashford to Faversham
road, but in a roomy Edwardian or late-Victorian house. The
mother and father were in their middle years, and there were three
daughters, attractive in varying styles, the youngest still a schoolgirl.
The one son, Jack, was an Oxford undergraduate, not encountered
until a fine evening during a Long Vacation when he came walking
up Kennington Lees with a fellow undergraduate called Rodney
Phillips, we somehow anticipating him near the step Kate had
failed to donkey-stone. He and Rodney (subsequently the founder
of a smart highbrow magazine called *Polemic*, and a book publisher)
were in some disbelief that close to the Clark family house could

84

actually reside a contributor to *New Writing*, as, in a way that now seems baffling, had been reported to them.

I had thought this was the Long Vacation of 1937, in which case the contribution in question would have been the smiling moustaches piece, inadequate trigger for their mild awe. But on reflection I see it was more likely 1938, when earlier in the year *New Writing* had published a poem of mine dedicated to the dead Maurice Stott. In that event Jack may well have actually just come down from Oxford. In the manner detested by some critics of *Souvenirs*, I leave the matter open, though I could easily ask him, for we became friends, and have remained so; he one of the noble band of close readers who do not compete at all in the creative field. Of course, the question also arises whether his memory would be more reliable than mine.

But if the later date is right I have rather prematurely reached the summer in whose ghastly maturity came the Munich crisis, which, before being resolved by Chamberlain's piece of paper bearing the worthless (as it turned out) Hitler signature, had led us to decide that Kate and our infant son should go to Blackpool, to her parents, in case war started suddenly and the bombers caught us in the south east with our pants down. The Spanish Civil War had done nothing to dispel the concept, fostered by such films as *Things to Come* (1936) and so completely depressing in those days, that civilians would be immediately under severe air attack when war arrived. Not long ago I came across a letter, somehow separated from its fellows, that I wrote to Kate in Blackpool during Munich days, saying I had been fitted for a respirator (as gas-masks were officially known) by Mrs "Y-cwt". "The thrill of a lifetime," I commented, with a facetiousness not diminishing over the years. The lady in question, in the Civil Defence organization, was the middle-aged wife of the village headmaster, Mr Exton.

Munich was late in the Ashford era: quite early was the arrival of a leaflet inviting subscriptions for a new "twice quarterly" periodical, *Twentieth Century Verse*. I sent my four shillings (20p) to the address named, 17 The Waldrons, Croydon, though not approving of the brief statement of editorial policy, which I judged poetically eclectic as well as politically uncommitted — to say nothing of the editorial address being unreassuringly non-metropolitan. As I write this, I take from the shelf the first number of the magazine, and see with surprise it is dated as late as January 1937. There must have been a longer gap than I recall between its appearance and the leaflet. Perhaps the editor, Julian Symons, was accumulating financial resources (i.e. saving a few pounds from his wages as secretary in the Victoria Street offices of some engineering companies). He says in his autobiographical *Notes From Another Country* (1972) that the leaflet brought in only nine subscriptions.

That first number did not allay the doubts raised in me by the leaflet. It opened with a poem by Dylan Thomas ("It is the sinners' dust-tongued bell"), a poet already a *bête noir* of mine. A poem by the editor was called "The Romantic Speaking": this, coupled with his name, conveyed some wispy figure more like an ineffectual Nineties poet than someone able to stand up to the rigours of the Thirties and the probably even more rigorous Forties. I was surprised when I met, as I did quite soon, a tough-minded six-footer; subsequent meetings gradually revealing a notable eater and drinker, expert table tennis and snooker player, cricketing days not long over. Even his name proved really to be Julius (as was Kingsford's, the founding father of Kingsford, Flower and Pain, always striking me as that of some powerfully astute character), enterprisingly changed by himself; and he had been familiarly known by the sporting youth of Clapham (the place of his family house) by a contraction of his second name, Gus. As to my own name, my few published poems had appeared above the moniker R. B. FULLER, on the lines of my Blackpool shingle. Soon, with his concern for nomenclature, Julian wrote: "Unless it is Reginald, you ought to use your first name." I followed his advice, as I have usually done down to this day, though he is likely to proffer it only infrequently.

Our first meeting was not awfully far from the flat occupied by Mervyn's mother and step-father, though the ambience was sharply contrasted, being a pub close, perhaps next door, to the Victoria Palace. I had been given a lift up, was to be given a lift back, late at night, by Kingsford's cashier, out on some spree with a small party. I rather think Ruthven Todd turned up at the pub; certainly Gavin Ewart came later to Julian's basement room in Pimlico, a locale favoured by him in other epochs, also. I have a feeling I encountered Hugh Gordon Porteous and D. S. Savage on that occasion, but that a meeting with H. B. Mallalieu was postponed till later. All were familiar names, contributors to *Twentieth Century Verse*.

And as I write this, in the late summer of 1980, the whole lot except Ruthven are still alive. Porteous, a man of letters of the highest standards, must now have achieved a tidy age (though in one's own old age one is inclined to exaggerate that of others). Gavin Ewart and H. B. Mallalieu, in those days respectively toughly and darkly handsome, both fell off writing verse, then returned to it in later life, Gavin with widely acknowledged success. Derek Savage abandoned verse for criticism, then more or less abandoned all writing; sustained by disciplines of faith, and perhaps diet, in actual living. Ruthven died not long ago, after years of ill-health brought on by cigarettes, booze and variable, usually insufficient, supplies of money. His parrot and jackdaw ways used to offend my Lancastrian puritanism. In the Auden style of the time he turned out many a poem about "history" or some hero of art or letters, like Klee. And soon after the outbreak of war, in the Café Royal, he read a poem I was showing to Julian for possible publication in a pamphlet called "Some Poems in Wartime", a sweeping-up mainly of left-overs from *Twentieth Century Verse*, a war casualty, and plagiarised it in a piece called "Various Ends" (though it must be admitted that the theme — poets' horrid fates — was eventually to some extent embodied by him in actuality; besides, my own poem was suspiciously like J. C. Ransom's "Survey of Literature", which nevertheless I always maintained I had not then read).

However, this rather too practical homage was a natural expression of Ruthven's possessive love for imaginative art and letters, and their practitioners. On the whole his work vacillated between the too hastily produced and the inordinately delayed. I remember seeing decades ago a notebook of his on fungi with beautiful drawings (he had been trained as an artist), then hearing not long before his death that plans were afoot to publish a book made out of this material, yet to appear. Even earlier, probably at the beginning of the war, I expressed admiration of a large notebook he had, bound in yellow buckram. He said he had found and bought a cache of good but cheap paper, had it bound up into a number of notebooks. He opened the one he was carrying, to demonstrate the paper's quality. His small, shapely handwriting covered the unruled page, save for a generous margin left for addenda and corrigenda, at the foot of which he had entered the running total of words written. How enviable and impressive I found this scrupulous professionalism, and what a contrast to my ugly, commercial "Memoranda and Minute Book"!

Ruthven survived into the epoch of excessively long hair for men, and I saw him two or three times (he lived mainly abroad) with unbecoming grey Lisztian locks, though his image in earlier years is more vivid — hair by no means short and always ruffled, but black, like plumage, matching the rims of his gig-lamps, big even before the fashion for big spectacles came in. He chain-smoked, dragging at his cig in quick snatches so as to retain command of the conversation. His phenomenally narrow visage was rightly emphasised by Julian, as early as the latter's first crime novel, written before the war, where Ruthven is cast as the murderer.

I shouldn't think I adequately showed my gratitude to Julian for his troubling in gathering Ruthven and the others (though encountering my literary peers more or less for the first time made a strong mark), any more than I did to John Lehmann, who about this time also took the initiative in establishing friendship. I review my personality with no more pleasure than my verse.

But thinking back to Ashford days usually brings pictures far removed from jaunts to the London literary underworld — or, what my mind was full of, despite being suddenly out of politics, anxiety over world events and the state of England. I see the limes of Kennington Lees astonishingly holding their golden leaves far into the autumn, utterly unlike Blackpool trees, such few as existed being blasted by the gales of September. I see my son in his "high" chair, probably no more than a year old, insomniac, his restlessness best assuaged by being brought in to overlook the bridge table — where Mervyn would be playing, the fourth probably Jack Clark; if not, as unknown to me now as the "third" to the author of "The Waste Land". And I "see", of the gramophone records bought then, those of the Busch Quartet playing Beethoven's Opus 131, and the young Ella Fitzgerald singing "Deep in the Heart of the South", persisting mélange of taste I never thought unusual. The time there, as measured by the calendar several months less than three years, seems because of personal and public happenings, of huge amplitude, especially compared with the flickering by of seasons in old age.

My job at Kingsford's was not so arduous that it immediately altered the character I had so far brought to the law. The firm had spilled over the adjoining building, but only on the second floor, where a communicating door had been opened, rather like the dormitories in Seafolde House. My office was the farthermost in the adjoining building, so remote that to save clients a trek I would see them, if it were vacant, in an antedeluvian room on the ground floor, nominally used by the Clerk to the West Ashford Rural District Council, whose job, however, seemed even less arduous than mine. On the way to my room I had to pass through one occupied by the cashier and a couple of junior clerks, and here I might linger for a chat or, while the craze lasted, a game of cricket played with an ebony ruler and, much to my timid taste, a crumpled-paper ball. Back in my own room I expect I devoted time to composing the pieces which were eventually a "feature" of the March 1938 number of *Twentieth Century Verse*, though whether more time than to office cricket may be doubted, for when Julian proposed the feature I had to scrape the bottom of the barrel for sufficient poems.

I say "my own room", but I shared it with the articled clerk, Frank Flower's son. That I wrote poetry in his presence seems unlikely — it would have been too conspicuous a demonstration of the firm's money going down the drain. In any event, my period there coincided with his statutory year at law school, possibly also a spell at Gibson and Weldon's, so I saw less of him than might be imagined. He was, or had been, known in the family as "Boy"; old playmates, like the Clark children (I believe our knowing the Clarks was through the Flowers), referred to him as "Bertie". However, his proper name was Richard, and that is what I called him. Even at nineteen or so he had the flair for the law, and for pleasing clients, possessed by his father. I had to represent in the Ashford police court a pilot of the First World War on a drugs charge, to which there was no defence. Richard wrote out the heads of my mitigation plea with such an acute sense of what would properly touch the heartstrings that Sir Charles Igglesden's bench let the defendant off lightly, and Sir Charles's newspaper quite amply reported the proceedings.

When he was free, Richard drove me to the police and county courts of Kent and East Sussex in his father's Triumph Roadster, a fast and dashing soft-top. I marvel now that Frank owned it: he may also have possessed a more sober vehicle, but memory does not report it. I can feel now the wind blowing through the car's side curtains, chilling my neck, already chilled by the stiff wing collar I sometimes did not bother to change out of after a county court appearance; the beautiful countryside, so novel, flying past. I liked Richard: what he made of me, impossible to conjecture. I see him now (a thought I would not have had in those days, taking English virtues for granted, certainly to be carried forward to a communist society) as representative of the best in the solicitors' profession (for he duly qualified, with a rare First Class in the Intermediate

Examination). Probably with equal glibness I also took for granted professional independence, and the law's generation of its own idealism, despite cynicism about the apparatus of bourgeois rule implanted by Terry Warnock. In the war to come Richard joined the Royal Marines, was severely wounded, won the M.C. Like Jack Clark, he was a fine cricketer.

The contrast with my own character and career need not be laboured. Why off my own bat hadn't I hit the magistrates and journalists for six in the drugs case? Lack of a true interest, of the common touch, of the energy to avoid the merely routine where the merely routine would serve — all these reasons might be advanced, yet perhaps the truth was vaguer: in fine, the Vamp Till Ready syndrome once more. Some day I should have a job in the law — or a literary standing — which would allow my selfhood fully to express itself. It was still, however, a blend of the cocky and the shy: the former underwritten by brain power of sorts; the latter made more of a handicap, in business matters at least, by gross diffidence about exercising authority. (It comes to me that this diagnosis was just as applicable in subsequent times).

Nevertheless, in advocacy, as in other sides of a solicitor's life, I couldn't help improving. Did the police court clients get their three guineas worth? Hard to say. I had a case at Hythe, a small dairy farmer charged with watering his milk, arising out of a routine check by the Ministry inspector. I believed in his innocence, and I don't think I was deceived (as I was about a client accused of careless driving, even though noting his red face: when I pressed a prosecution witness on some point it was plain the defendant was lucky not to have been charged with drunken driving). The line of watered milk cases made it almost impossible to rebut the presumption of guilt if the specific gravity test were positive: phenomenally wet pastures, careless washing of churns, malicious employee — such, as I recall, were about all the defences that had succeeded, and themselves of a fundamental implausibility, needing convincing evidence. The test had not been far on the wrong side, and the farmer made a good witness. But in a sense the very scrupulosity of his procedures with the milk, which I elicited from him, precluded possible defences. What I should have done (I realised, brooding unhappily after the event) was to invite the bench, in the strongest terms, if they believed his denial of dilution, to acquit my client despite the *res ipsa loquitur* line of cases (heavily relied on, of course, by the Ministry prosecution). No doubt if Richard had been writing my heads of submission he would have got me effectively to quote: "when you have eliminated the impossible, whatever remains, *however impossible*, must be the truth" — the reason, though hidden, outside the accused's control or intent.

As one often in the police court, I became known to the Ashford Superintendent of Police, a rather Goeringlike figure (that individual, as head of the German airforce, being then much in the public mind), fat and jolly but, as one conceived it, not jolly all through. He once gave me a lift back from an outlying magistrates' court where we had both been appearing; at least one stop on the way, at the premises of an obsequious publican, confirming the view of the police taken by *State and Revolution*. I rode in a police-car on another occasion when the Superintendent sent for me at lunchtime at home to bring me to the cells, where a young man charged with rape had asked for a solicitor. There was to be a special sitting of the magistrates that afternoon. The story my new client unfolded seemed one of family fantasy, his accuser being his sister-in-law, senior in years, whose appearance in the witness-box — sallow, nervous, agitated — bore out what the accused had told me. In cross-examination I ploughed on through what without cliché might have been called sordid details, conscious of the woman on the Bench of three, the chairman of which, on that occasion, I think was no less than the owner or tenant-for-life of Eastwell Park, not at all playing the effete role ascribed to such personae in my ballad in that "special feature" of *Twentieth Century Verse*. The magistrates threw the case out, persuaded by my argument that there was insufficient corroboration of the kind required by law. Perhaps the Superintendent prosecuted with only moderate enthusiasm.

Why didn't I use knowledge of this kind in the fiction attempted before the war? And, indeed, after? To advance the Vamp Till Ready syndrome again will hardly do. As a matter of fact I was greatly interested in both crime fiction and true crime cases, but though I eventually wrote a few crime novels they exploited scarcely at all the interesting actualities of the criminal side of things. As I write this, I recall an almost Dostoevskyan scene following an inquest where I had been representing a man whose wife had been killed and his child injured by a motorist who had knocked them down while they were bicycling along a country road. The evidence against the motorist brought out by my questioning proved so damning (among other things, he had not stopped) that the jury returned a verdict of manslaughter against him, though I had had almost entirely in mind my client's claim against the motorist's insurance company. At the end of the winter's afternoon-long hearing, the lights having come on in the courtroom like some *coup de théâtre*, the police had to make an arrest on the spot. Alas, the circumstantial detail and even the feeling-tone have gone beyond fiction's recapture, though it is always surprising how little of both ingredients from reality fiction needs.

I could have soldiered on with Kingsford's. In the long term I may well not have minded the life of a country-town solicitor, probably a partner, early quitting the sixteen shilling flat, even moving into what Mervyn often pointed out, as we drove with him in his little red sports car, using a phrase my Oldham and Blackpool ears had possibly never heard before, "a lovely old house." But I was still intent on living in London, which I may have seen as a condition precedent to literary achievement — not through metropolitan back-scratching (which any way I have never found to exist) — but to the young provincial's deep and well-attested, if not entirely rational, desire to be up-to-date and at the heart of cultural action. It could also have been that I wanted to escape from private practice, like (as I learnt much later from his letters, and with whom I do not compare myself in any deep sense) Wallace Stevens, and for the same reasons. I do not remember when I started applying for jobs again — perhaps quite late in Ashford days, even not until after Munich. And I do not think I put in more than two or three applications before success came.

The respirator letter previously referred to also makes naive yet now enigmatic allusion to my view that England was lined up with the "wrong people" and that it would be necessary to "resist". I shall briefly return to the question of political attitudes to the events of 1938 and 1939, but I pause here to note how mysterious in retrospect seems one's relationship to large contemporary issues, casting doubt on any comparatively simple attitude revealed by these and other memoirs.

The cup of Munich passed, my wife and son soon returned. A memorable feature of the crisis was the house lights coming on one evening in the Odeon cinema — or, perhaps, more dramatically, merely the footlights that illuminated the curtains hiding the blank screen — and the cinema manager appearing from the wings to announce the Ashford Air Raid Precautions Officer. Then entered Swann, of Poncia, Swann and Carter. As a matter of fact, the errant nose was not a great feature of his appearance: he was personable, married to a good-looking girl, and lived in a white stucco house Mervyn might well have put into his approved category. Swann gave a good account of himself in this quite early instance of the disagreeable impingement of world events on cosy English private life. (Soon after writing this, at the end of the 1980 summer, I saw in the *Law Society's Gazette*, a paper in which time's blades are not infrequently concealed, that he had just died, aged 81).

The "Minute Book" already described is deficient in poems, probably sparse any way, of 1938. It contains no draft or fair copy, for instance, of a piece that survived into my *Collected Poems* of 1962 (a premature volume, for with more stuff to collect a more rigorous attitude to omissions could have been maintained), written during a holiday at St Mary's Bay in Kent with H. B. Mallalieu, his wife and son, and Julian Symons; Jack Clark also coming for a day. *Souvenirs* mentions Julian's to me awe-inspiring literary industry on that occasion. Herbert Mallalieu also impressed me by showing me a small notebook with close-ruled lines, which he said he had chosen for poems since it simulated how the verse would look when printed, and so he could better judge its effectiveness. Julian certainly, Herbert probably, wrote far more than I did on that curious *ad hoc* holiday in a furnished bungalow. Indeed, I feel sure that apart from a few impromptu lines resulting from a literary game, the only work I turned out was the poem before mentioned, written, with a wrong-headed or cloth-eared attempt at novelty, in nine-line stanzas, which eventually appeared in a now-forgotten little magazine called *Seven*. A crux in this poem was the line: "The penis lighthouse standing." To make sense, the quotation should be amplified:

> Aeroplanes softly landing
> Beyond the willowed marsh:
> The penis lighthouse standing
> Aloof with rolling eye
> From shingle flat and harsh . . .

I was not happy with penis, though moderately descriptive. For one thing, a George Barker poem had already used the noun adjectivally in the phrase "the penis waterpistol"; for another, the medical/obscene connotation offended me in the context. Doubtful, moreover, if it can be maintained that the organs in question have *rolling* eyes, though that epithet may have been introduced after I had changed the other epithet to "sexy", the latter word not ideal but better then than after forty years of continuing debasement. What the lighthouse was more like (the one at Dungeness) was a vinegar bottle with a perforated ceramic attachment to its cork, enabling the acetic fluid to be sprinkled over a plate or newspaper of fish-and-chips. I remember Wetton, in a plum-coloured suit, on the boarders' usual Saturday night out, using such an object when, shaking in my shoes, I first visited a chip-shop from Seafolde House, emporia of that kind being strictly out of bounds. Could that evident *flâneur* and *bon viveur* really have been biffed by Waller's father?

A great difference between poetry in St Mary's Bay times and now would be the present likelihood of the actual vinegar-bottle being worked in, though of course the poet of today, using *vers libre*, would not face difficulties of rhyme, line-length, and succinctness. Also, as to increasing informality, I recall being doubtful (though pleased) when Julian proposed to print in *Twentieth Century Verse* my contribution to the verse-writing game (which I think was to write within a time limit a poem beginning "To murder someone").

> To murder someone was his childish dream
> Achieved by proxy on the silver screen.
> Later a rape was all his dark attention
> And this was done by primitive invention.
> His crimes more trivial as he older grew:
> He ended up by being me and you.

The shaky syntax of the penultimate line, the question whether in the last line "me" should not more properly be "I" — these were continuing botherations. What strong confirmation in all this of one's feebleness still, in those (and later) days; feebleness time and experience have alleviated but by no means cured.

Quite apart from the poems therein, an unlikable thing about the "Minute Book" is the handwriting, sloping excessively to the right. Not long after, when I had seen and been impressed by the orthography of Julian and of Ruthven, it became a good deal smaller, sometimes comically so. It never achieved Julian's fineness, however, for one thing because I lacked his gift for finding pens with that capacity (at one epoch a *glass* pen). During the war it quite suddenly became almost upright. I used to put that down to having to write legible airgraphs when abroad in the Navy (the airgraph was photographically reduced in size in the country of dispatch, and went through the mails in that form), but I believe now it reflected some psychological change. Cessation of guilt? Expiation? The Nelson touch? Modest literary success? *Quien sabe?* (as D. H. Lawrence, impressively to me in my nonage, used to put in his letters).

I'm reminded of a time at school when I was twelve or so. A day master (in fact, he did not even come in to lunch, but thriftily ate sandwiches at his form-room desk), who signed himself in tremendously neat upright handwriting, joining all the initials ingeniously together, "W.S.G.P" or "W.S. G. Proctor" or even "W.S. Groveham Proctor" (the last-mentioned cognomen being impressive, despite his just nickname being "Cherry Nose"), once called me up to the aforesaid desk and asked me if my eyesight was all right. I was flattered at the acknowledgment of my physical persona, though compelled to reply in the affirmative. "You see you don't write on the lines," he said. Strangely enough, Cherry Nose reappears in this narration.

Looking back, I realise that as a youth and young man I was never satisfied with my handwriting, though sometimes regarding it with indulgent affection. The attitude was not far from that I had towards my verse. I believe that they continuously improved over the years. I quite see that others may prefer earlier periods, in both departments, but would stick sanguinely to my view.

As stated, I stopped using the "Minute Book" regularly in September 1937. I returned to it early in 1939, starting a satire in couplets, wisely abandoned, and drafting a few other poems. By then we had moved from Kennington to Blackheath, in south-east London. My mother's Graves' disease had at last been diagnosed, and she also came to London, temporarily, to undergo a partial thyroidectomy. The surgeon whose speciality was this then severe operation, held a consultancy at the London Hospital in the Whitechapel Road. I visited there before and after the surgery. Details of the journey have passed from memory, though I must have gone under the Thames by bus through the Blackwall Tunnel, thence by tram. I see the hospital, faintly Grecian, black with dirt — like the Lancastrian public buildings of my boyhood — and my mother sitting up in bed in the lighted ward, wearing a "bed-jacket", probably crocheted by herself. The loss of weight and browning of the skin were so classically symptomatic that to her amusement colour photographs had been taken of her, a technical process not so commonplace then as now. Perhaps they even appeared in some medical journal or textbook. Post-operatively, she was in danger, not conscious during my visit. Later she said she had felt then as though falling into a dark pit, being pulled out again and again.

One of those last poems in the "Minute Book" contains the following passage:

> I went underground at Whitechapel;
> In the lavatory by the hospital
> I farted and the man beside me laughed.
> "The other night, down the Commercial Road,
> I wanted to break wind and did,
> And two young women passing said *Just listen*
> *To that old man*," he said and laughed again,
> Not old or drunk . . .

Could I possibly have used the incident of my Gibson and Weldon days to vivify what seems an otherwise verisimilitudinous poem? Or did the episode in fact take place in 1939, myself not present at the girls' auditory experience? The circumstantial mention of the Commercial Road favours the latter proposition, but the truth remains in doubt.

7　The Equitable

> *It has been said that Mr Ruegg's [a local poet, fl 1890] intellect should have been given entirely to literary work instead of being spent upon sanitary science, but no mind can be degraded by devotion to those pursuits which give health and happiness to the people.*
>
> — Vincent's Records of the Woolwich District

Another myth that must have gradually formed in my mind as the years rolled by was that my first book of poems came out before the war. In fact, as with slight surprise I recently discovered, it was published in December 1939. Only in the nick of time was I saved from being for ever labelled a Forties poet. I expect I was also sweating on the top line at the prospect of passing yet another birthday (my twenty-eighth on 11 February 1940) without having produced a first collection. With the example before me of Dylan Thomas and a good few others, I felt I was elderly to be gestating still. Publication, even of a fugitive kind, was not easily achieved in that era: it was Julian Symons, ever enterprising and professional, who found a publisher not only for himself but also for his friends — Gavin Ewart, D. S. Savage, me. I expect we had all tried and failed in orthodox channels: what Julian introduced us to was the Fortune Press, hitherto known, if known at all, as publisher of a few scholarly editions, and of more dubious, though one would guess scarcely more readable, works of eroticism and demonology.

Blake Morrison, in his recent learned book *The Movement*, describes L. Caton as "head of the Fortune Press", but though strictly correct the words may mislead. I doubt if the Press had any staff at all — except possibly a typist, for I recall once getting a letter from Caton, typed quite well on a machine with strangely large type. On a sole occasion also, I met Caton, in the basement of the Fortune Press premises (or, more likely, the basement that comprised the premises) in the Buckingham Palace Road. Julian was with me: I think Caton had expressed to him a wish to meet the author he had published or was about to. I remember nothing of that encounter except seeing on the basement floor large numbers of unbound copies of the Press' publications; not an auspicious augury, as it strikes me now. Did Julian report to me, or did I myself observe it on that occasion, Caton nudging with his boot a pile of, say, *Fourteen, a Diary of the Teens, by a Boy*, and remarking: "Good stock"? — a phrase that crept into family usage for goods injudiciously or too abundantly purchased.

My arrangement with Caton was tacit, and I have never regarded it as other than reasonable: I paid him nothing and he paid me nothing. Other authors of his, like Kingsley Amis and Philip Larkin, were miffed at not getting money out of him, but theirs was a later epoch and they became writers whose books were popular. I have no idea how many copies were printed or sold of my *Poems* (the foolishly neutral title almost obligatory for a first collection, in light of the example set by Auden and Spender). At some time further copies must have been taken from the basement to the binder, for I have seen the book in a case different from the original biblical black. In either state it is a satisfactorily rare book. The late Cyril Connolly once told me he had tried to get it for his collection of first books, and I promised to send him a copy if I had a spare, but when I searched I seemed to possess only one. (The promise was made on a comparatively genial occasion — after dinner, in John Julius Norwich's house, after I had received the Duff Cooper Memorial Prize for 1968. In lieu of *Poems*, I sent Cyril a copy of the beautiful pamphlet my son and daughter-in-law had printed on their hand press as a surprise for my sixtieth birthday. What was no surprise was that Cyril did not bother to acknowledge it, for he almost always seemed to me difficult and supercilious. Yet I must add that the last time I saw him, at his publisher's party in 1973 for his book *The Evening Colonnade*, he took what for him could be called pains to be forthcoming and agreeable. Perhaps he had premonitions of mortality).

Since writing the foregoing, Timothy D'Arch Smith's illuminating article "R. A. Caton and the Fortune Press" has appeared in the *Times Literary Supplement* (September 12, 1980) — but best,

I think, to leave what I originally said, and amend and amplify a little from Mr D'Arch Smith's research. I am reminded that Caton "had published a little poetry at the very beginning — T. W. H. Crosland, Cecil Day-Lewis and Lord Alfred Douglas". The Day-Lewis book was that poet's first, *Beechen Vigil and other poems* (1925). It would seem likely that my visit to the Press was to premises in Belgrave Road, which Caton had acquired at the outbreak of war — premises opened up by Mr D'Arch Smith in 1970 during Caton's last illness and found to contain "good stock" in staggering quantities. It also appears that Caton himself was the typist of my letter from the Press, for the *TLS*, trying to obtain payment of a long-outstanding account for advertising (see Mr Bruce Coward's letter in the *TLS* of September 26, 1980), put the bailiffs in the Belgrave Road premises, and they seized Caton's "old and treasured typewriter, the only object of any value they could find". And presumably Caton's initials *were* "R. A.".

I was pleased and excited about the publication of *Poems*, though it was attended by worries that now appear ludicrous. For instance, one had to be content with the poems running-on instead of each starting on a fresh page, seeming a grave aesthetic sin (though now rather favoured by me as keeping the cost down without succumbing to that *minceur* character books of verse often today assume). And when the volume was at last in my hands and I slipped off the dust jacket, I saw to my horror that along the spine, between ROY FULLER and POEMS, was not a dot or asterisk or other printer's device I should have considered satisfactory, but a hyphen.

The time factor may have been even more of an anxiety than previously indicated, for my book was not reviewed with Julian's *Confusions About X*, or Gavin Ewart's *Poems and Songs* or Derek Savage's *The Autumn World*, but with subsequent "Fortune Poets" (as Caton's slight publicity tagged us) — Glyn Jones and Henry Treece; uncongenial figures not, so far as I know, promoted by Julian. However, any delay in publication of that kind need only have been of the order of weeks to alter reviewing companions. To speak of reviews at all is a bit misleading, for I doubt if there were as many as half a dozen, the war having put paid to a few little magazines that might have augmented this meagre sum. One of the reviews was in *John o' London's Weekly*, in terms a good deal less encouraging than those in which its editor had once written to me when, as a schoolboy, I used to submit short stories. The reviewer was Herbert E. Palmer, born exactly a hundred years ago, in 1880, not unknown to verse anthologies of a former day. He ended his notice:

> What most of our new poets do not seem to understand is this: If you took all the most curious lines and phrases of Shakespeare and strung them together to make complete poems you would perpetrate metrical monstrosities; and if God took half a dozen pairs of human eyes (even the most lovely) and stuck them all into one human face, everybody would flee from it, and the little children would run screaming in terror down the street.

As a matter of fact, I had recently reviewed a prose work by Herbert Palmer, *Post-Victorian Poetry* — in rude fashion — in *Twentieth Century Verse*, so I could not be heard to complain. Also, I had actually seen him, pointed out to me (or perhaps I recognized him from his photographs) on some occasion I am stumped to identify — for I would have said I never went to literary parties until latish in the war, when John Lehmann began to ask me to his. Palmer seemed aged to me, though then no more than sixty, and indeed his wild hair was quite white; and an aura of irascibility and disappointment seemed to surround his stringy figure.

So no danger of the reviews making me known in the Woolwich Equitable Building Society as the author of a book of verse of (in Palmer's hyperbolic phrase) "extreme Modernism", with consequent risk to my legal career. I say that not wholly facetiously, though I probably claimed "literary ability" as a qualification when applying for the job as an assistant solicitor with the society. I think the phrase had become a ploy, like the "extremely interested" opening of my workless days. The advertisement in the *Law Society's Gazette* to which I responded did not mention "building society", merely "large corporate body", and was no more topographically specific than "south-east London". The advertisement was of a new post; inserted by A. E. Shrimpton, who six or seven years before had set up the society's own legal department, in origin the hiving-off of the society's business from the practice of a Woolwich firm of solicitors. The society had indeed, during the Twenties and Thirties, grown into a "large corporate body" — the Solicitor's Department, as it was commonly called, employed a staff of sixty or seventy, representing what in those days would have been a substantial private practice.

100

Apart from a trivial feature of our first encounter to be mentioned later, I do not know why Fred Shrimpton chose me out of the good few applicants for what looked quite a promising post. He never really came clean when in later years I might joke about his irrationality and my luck, though he once told me of the trouble he had had with another interviewee — just the sort of confrontation under non-Queensberry Rules he detested. This rejected applicant was so irate that he pressed for the decision in my favour to be reversed, and even enlisted the help of an eminent figure known both to him and someone among the society's directors or senior management. Hearing this, thinking of one's own inferior qualifications, one could not but feel guilty, though that emotion Fred was far from intending to induce with his revelation so many years *ex post facto*.

Pressure of the foregoing kind would only have stiffened his resolve, for he also detested dirty work at the crossroads, just as he detested anyone who "put on the dog". I worked with him for twenty years, admiration unslackening, never once having even a tiff with him. But I must try not to look forward too much from that pre-National Service period of association with the Equitable, beginning with the day in the autumn of 1938 when I went to Woolwich for my first interview. The journey from Ashford was not arduous. I would simply change at London Bridge or (less cleverly) Charing Cross (both stations of intense familiarity in years to come, neither possessing beauty nor even comfort). A crisis arose when the local train stopped at Woolwich Dockyard. Should I alight? Topographical perspectives, so far as could be seen, seemed inauspicious, and the stomachic worms of anxiety were somewhat allayed by the train soon arriving at Woolwich Arsenal, where I did get out. Equitable House, the society's chief office, quite recently built, its Portland stone still pale, was opposite the station. I had time to spare, wandered by chance into the street market between Equitable House and the Georgian entrance to the Royal Arsenal. I expect I found on that occasion the market's only bookstall for I have always had a nose for such things, even having repeated dreams of bookstalls and bookshops of such circumstantiality that I have sometimes when awake fleetingly wondered if they did not truly exist in some town visited in the past. The Woolwich Market stall was run by the same fellow during my thirty-one years (as it turned out) of working daily in Woolwich, though he did not last as long as me, and his stall disappeared with him. Far from young even before the war, in the end he looked very frail. No more amiable to me than was Cyril Connolly, he was even less so to the ignorant who asked him questions, or to the over-sanguine who tried to reverse roles and sell him books. Though his stock changed slowly, I often used to look it over, there being a paucity of intellectual recreation in Woolwich — sometimes out of guilt or pity buying a book I did not really want, such as a volume of Richard Le Gallienne's literary journalism, many years later passed on to the London Library. The vendor (whose name I never knew) once said to me — one of his rare remarks, muttered through a ragged, stained moustache under a nose not surprisingly dew-dropped in the east wind frequently blowing across the market square — "I've educated half Woolwich." But our exchanges were usually mere nods.

On that first walk round the market I certainly found, among the stalls, the public lavatory, where I had a "wash and brush-up" for 3d or even 2d; the service including a small clean towel in a paper sleeve. The soap was liquid, in a container difficult of access, and strong, pungent, almost redolent of the fluid used to disinfect the bogs at Seafolde House. Nevertheless, I washed my face, improving appearance and morale; a touch, indeed, that would appeal to Fred Shrimpton, as will appear. I was wearing my suit of darkish brown Manx tweed, made by a small gents' outfitter in Ashford. I say "made", but nothing on the Frank Flower or even Harold E. Pain lines is to be envisaged: the operation was not carried out on the premises but by a remoter organization serving such establishments. I had obviously not then come across the dictum that gentlemen do not wear brown suits — as persuasive but perhaps no more reliable than Curzon's saying gentlemen do not have soup at luncheon.

Nevertheless, the suit was a success, not least its material, ordered from a swatch of samples the proprietor had got in after my insistence on a cloth sober but soft — as (it was in my mind) worn by Aldous Huxley in the West End. That the suiting eventually found to fill this bill was Manx tweed conferred an added cachet. Somewhat mysterious why this should be, for neither my mother's voyagings to the Isle of Man nor our holidays there in earlier days had discovered any elegant life, rather the reverse (as in the case of Bone's father's alleged use of his cess-pit, referred to in *Souvenirs*). I still wore the suit after the war, when two or three moth holes had been invisibly mended: amazing art; lost now, I suppose, or priced beyond the thrifty market most requiring it.

102

I was taken in to Fred Shrimpton by his secretary. On the way we heard the rapid, expressionless voice of one engaged in "examining" an abstract of title. I made some such feeble but amiable comment as the curious sound being a universal feature of solicitor's offices, so that entering Fred's room we were both grinning. I saw later that in the light of Fred's character no better entry could have been made, particularly if that day he had already had a heavily serious interview with the applicant who proved so aggressive eventually. Fred was not in the least lacking in courage (in the First War he had been both a motor-cycle dispatch-rider and a machine-gunner), but preferred life not to include unnecessary clashes of will. One of the lessons my impatient nature did its best to learn from him in the practice of the law was the inherent capacity of a problem to, as he often phrased it, "work itself out" — not that he was in the least a dilatory lawyer. Indeed, I should add that in soundness and accuracy I never knew his equal.

Against the room's light oak panelling (Equitable House was a compendium of Thirties middle-of-the-road styles) I saw a man slightly below medium height, in his early forties, of extreme neatness in dress and hair-style. He was always pretty fit; at this time, after being a fine tennis player, just developing an alternative interest in golf. His questioning would have been measured and methodical, but I think it quite soon became plain that a deal was likely to be on. Superficially, the job seemed mainly concerned with conveyancing (and, of course, building society law) but fairly unpredictable chores arose out of the society's diurnal existence, the full extent of which, of course, I did not discover until I had moved in. Fred was the only solicitor in the department, though in a private practice of that size there would have been several partners. He was never a shirker, but some tasks he found distasteful and wanted help of a kind only a qualified man could provide. He had a number of excellent unadmitted managing clerks in the department, but he plainly felt, in some not entirely obscure way, that it would be an advantage to have a fellow at hand used to defending in cases of rape and watered milk. One example of such usefulness, merely notional, I fear, I will soon give an account of.

It might have been that very afternoon I met the remaining four of the society's senior executives, though more likely an occasion was specially arranged for them to give me the once-over before my appointment was clinched. At that epoch the senior executives had a sit-down tea round a large table in the smaller of the two committee

103

rooms on the boardroom floor. Bread-and-butter and jam, cakes and biscuits, were the order of the day. The amenity impressed me, like others in Equitable House such as the built-in letter-chute running the height of the building, ending in a Post Office controlled post-box on the lower-ground floor, apertures for posting letters conveniently extant on every floor. The communal tea-taking custom survived the war for a spell: it ended just about the time the aforesaid apertures had to be sealed up because of the chute being periodically choked with unsuitably-sized letters. Thus and in other small ways was marked the coming of an era of rotting standards and growing indiscipline.

I joined the executives for tea, whatever the date was. The General Manager and Secretary, T. R. Chandler, was an actuary, of eminence and experience in the building society world, had seen the society grow, helped its evolution. He was then coming up to retirement, grey, distinguished-looking, tallish. He said little, was always courteous but quite awesome. From most men affection and respect can be won: Tommy (not that I ever came to call him that) Chandler won them where possible, in the most natural way. How he fared with awkward bastards I do not know, but have little doubt he would triumph without change of style or tactics on his part. He knew what was going on in the deepest recesses of the society, even in the family lives of its staff. His handwriting was among the most remarkable I have known: modern computer lettering may be envisaged, but executed with idiosyncratic artistic delicacy. The Assistant General Manager was a sweet-natured man called Austin Smith, who had to go prematurely through ill-health, but whose cultivated nature luckily found compensations in retirement. Alexander Meikle, the Assistant Secretary, was a young Scottish chartered accountant, brought in to mechanize the society's accounting system, which by then he had done. The business-getting side of the organization, including the branches, then quite few, was under the dapper Agency Manager, Harold Codner, who, like Austin Smith, had been a very young aviator in the RFC during the 1914–18 war.

Perhaps even at that testing tea I observed the smoking habits of these four (I would have known something of Fred Shrimpton's from our interview), in those days before the weed had been linked with lung cancer a widespread, almost Dickensian indication of character. Chandler was not averse to a cigarette but preferred a pipe, and greatly enjoyed a cigar on a formal or semi-formal occasion. I have heard of him passing his tobacco-pouch unexpectedly to an underling, and believe its contents were invariably a mixture of Player's Gold Block and Balkan Sobranie. Austin Smith smoked Gold Flake cigarettes, popular during the 1914–18 war and persisting during the Thirties, the buttercup-coloured packet prominent in tobacconists'. The inside of the packet was, of course, white, but Stephen Spender may have come to feel there was some contradiction in the last stanza of his early poem, previously mentioned, about the unemployed friend:

Nor shall I ever fail to see
One photographic memory,
Of how, still leaning on a post,
You stride the gutter where men spit,

And, laughing loudly, we both look
Down on a torn and yellow box.
For on my brain I felt impress
That white, appalling emptiness.

After its publication in *Oxford Poetry 1930*, these last two stanzas of the poem were omitted (and, alas, the impact lessened by other revisions). I think Austin Smith himself gave up Gold Flake, but this would be because of a lung complaint prompting him to give up smoking in general.

Did Sandy Meikle already smoke Du Maurier, a tipped cigarette, in 1938? I am prepared to be contradicted, for Du Maurier, if extant then, must surely have been a new brand. He certainly smoked them solidly after the war (until renouncing smoking late in life), lighting them with matches (preferably non-safety), for he distrusted devices like petrol-lighters, propelling-pencils and pencil-sharpeners. Fred Shrimpton smoked Gold Flake when I first knew him, if not so devotedly as Austin: in any case, he did not inhale, and liked to smoke a cigar. Harold Codner was a Capstan, later a Players Medium man, which eventually Fred became, though I think I am right in saying both went over to Players Gold Leaf when after the war that cigarette was transmogrified by its manufacturers into a tipped cigarette. In his early eighties Fred became skittish about smoking, sometimes on, sometimes off: I believe Harold, who also lived into his eighties, was more faithful. What a pleasure I lost when I myself gave up smoking at the age of sixty-two!

A greater knowledge of those four colleagues of Fred's came after the war — even of T. R. Chandler, who continued as a member of the Board of Directors, and of Austin Smith, whom I saw sometimes after his retirement in 1946. A few all-too-human traits were revealed, not apparent in the briefer encounters of early days, but their standards of work and, above all, of personal dignity and integrity, were extremely high. Moreover, without any apparatus of consumer-protection statutes and organizations, all these senior managers were implicitly convinced of the mutuality of building societies, the equitable balance needing to be struck between the interests of borrowers and investors. It is not without significance that a few years before I arrived it had been decided, on a periodical revision of the society's rules, not to omit the clumsy "Equitable" from its title.

To start with I was gravelled to anatomize the evil role of building societies in an evil (and inadequate) capitalist economy, analysis not being helped, I suppose, by finding able and honest men running the Equitable. In the novel he wrote at this very time, *Coming Up For Air*, George Orwell faced the same problem, and solved it with his usual disregard for probability and fact. His invention, the Cheerful Credit Building Society, not only lends people money on mortgage: it owns the house-building company, the builders' merchants who supply the materials, and the company in which the freehold of the houses is vested. That these latter activities are contrary to law (as it is for building societies to distribute profits in the ordinary sense) is not taken account of by Orwell, who rampages on about his self-invented scandal in fascist (or at any rate demogogic) fashion.

The answer I came to myself was that building societies served the bourgeoisie by providing funds for speculative builders. There was also a collaborative practice between building society and builder that was soon to be challenged by the Left through the Courts in a quite dramatic way. A society was able to make mortgage advances of an extremely high percentage of the purchase price by taking collateral security on cash deposited with the society by the builder of the houses. The deposits were "pooled" to form security for numbers of mortgages, so that the cash deposit by the builder in any particular case did not need to be the full amount of the "excess" advance in that case.

The Equitable's financial year end was (and is) 30 September, so the annual general meeting was held just before Christmas. The first I attended (in the Chartered Insurance Institute in the City) came only a couple of weeks after I joined the Solicitor's Department, and, like much else at the time, made its mark. Once again, the provision of tea came into it. After the meeting this was provided for the big-wigs in a restaurant in the basement. I suppose Fred Shrimpton must have taken me down under his wing on that first occasion. After the war I used to make my own way there, but for years was unsure as to my entitlement, though never challenged. The cloakroom and lavatories were also in the basement: rather stricture-making to find oneself standing, without secure status, beside the Vice-Chairman of the Board, say, or even T. R. Chandler. After my first attendance at the AGM I started a short story in which some demented and out-of-work borrower, who has been evicted from his house by the mortgagee-building society, goes to the society's AGM and shoots the Chairman. Perhaps I am putting the plot in unfavourably stark terms, but could I ever have conceived such a narration seriously? It must be so, though I doubt if I ever finished it. A comic Kafkaesque account of the basement tea-tables and urinal-stalls would not have occurred to me as a more promising concept.

I ought to emphasise that the effects of the economic crisis of the start of the Thirties on building society borrowers was still quite marked. The man in charge of arrears, F. A. Wellman, of infinite compassion and patience, attended on T. R. Chandler first thing every day to report the situation. The department dealing with properties the society had had to take possession of was euphemistically named "Special Securities" and its head "Chief Clerk", mild humbug Orwell would have made much of. It may well have been the then "Chief Clerk" of whom it was first said that he put the "quit" in "Equitable". In some domestic speech after the war the saying drew a slight laugh when I applied it to a subsequent official on the arrears side, but the great days of moustache-twirling mortgagees had already gone. It should be said that the jest comes out better for knowing that the society was called by the local masses "the E*quit*able" (though advertising campaigns may now have succeeded in changing the usage to "the Woolwich") — just as Terry Warnock and Rose and others used to refer to the class enemy as ca*pit*alists. However jarring to those who know better, some justice in both pronunciations must be admitted, the latter seeming to imply a trivial, even disgusting urinatory, quality in the bourgeoisie.

107

How seriously did I take the role of building societies in sustaining the fabric of a society I regarded as doomed? Was there not much that was ludicrous and cowardly in becoming, with my views, even a junior executive in such an organization; in fact, in being a lawyer at all without professionally helping the underprivileged? Certainly one's spirit was divided, leading a life of outward conformity. The extreme opinions expressed to friends, even acquaintances, seem in retrospect mere parlour pinkism, of the feeblest kind. However, one is perhaps too inclined from this distance in time to play down one's resolution in face of the disasters that threatened, the hopes that glimmered. For instance, though Munich was an enormous relief it seemed clear that the time of testing of one's physical courage and ideology had been only a trifle postponed.

It never struck me with any force in those days that the building society was a characteristic British invention, still with strong elements of mutuality; no doubt benefitting its managers (managers as a new class was a notion just becoming fashionable) and those profiting from house-building, but part of the overwhelmingly well-conducted sector of trade unions and friendly societies. Almost simultaneously with my entry into the building society world came the notorious Borders case (did that prompt Orwell's exaggerations?) and the ensuing reforms and restrictions of the Building Societies Act 1939, the first building society legislation since 1894. The case arose through a combination of bad building, slap-dash legal work, an ill-worded builder's estate brochure, and a mortgage loan by a building society to the wife of a communist taxi-driver. Unlucky for the society involved, but the circumstances were by no means outré, and a fiction founded on them would have compared favourably with Orwell's bosh.

When Mrs Borders was sued by the building society for arrears she denied she had signed the mortgage deed produced. She counterclaimed for damages for fraudulent misrepresentation, alleging that the society and the builder were so closely associated that the society was responsible for statements in the builder's brochure about value for money and good workmanship. She argued that the society had no power to make the loan any way, because a substantial percentage of it was based on the additional security of the builder's pooled cash deposits, whereas the building societies statutes and the society's rules required the security to be wholly freehold or leasehold property, viz the house. The course of the litigation was complex, but it is roughly true to say that whereas the society prevailed on the points of fraud and the power to make the loan, Mrs Borders was the practical victor. At many of the court hearings she appeared in person, and her eloquence and acumen led her to be compared by the popular press with Portia, the society being tacitly cast in the role of Shylock.

In those days did I truly want Mrs Borders to win? The answer must be yes; greatly in doubt if asked today. I should still feel a similar *Schadenfreude* at seeing another society in the shit (one with standards less rigorous than the Equitable), but also pangs at blows struck at an order established for the people's good. Through his membership of the Legal Advisory Panel of the Building Societies Association, Fred Shrimpton was involved in the legislation following Borders, and collaborated in a book expounding it. A little of the work rubbed off on me (rather a turn up for the "literary ability" qualification) — a taste of something I did much more of twenty years on, and grew fond of; like falling for someone for ages merely grudgingly tolerated, as in a fiction by Charlotte Brontë or Daphne du Maurier.

I did not myself before the war become a mortgagor, though the society made loans to its staff at a privileged rate of interest, and I could have borrowed from my mother the relatively small deposit needed. What an investment a house bought in 1938 would have proved, if not flattened by Goering's men! But in a bohemian way — perhaps a hangover from the red trousers and the like of D. H. Lawrence-reading times — the idea of living in a modest suburban house, perhaps one of a row or pair, was anathema. The emotion may have been reinforced in an odd way by a mild Mervyn-induced lovely-old-house ambition. Our first dwelling in Blackheath was a maisonette, the first and second floors of an undistinguished late Victorian house in a wide but busy road linking the A2 with the A20. Our Ashford rent was about doubled, but then so was the space, which included an enormous sitting room and a main bedroom scarcely smaller. Heating facilities were minuscule. The winter of 1938–39 was severe, and the pipes froze (fairly rotten, at best). When they thawed, water fell on us in bed, though we were not sleeping on the top floor. I marvel at our youthful hardihood.

In the maisonette below (basement and ground floor) were two elderly sisters and the unmarried daughter of one of them. We put up at the windows of the main bedroom the Ashford curtains made for that purpose there. They were too short, as could be seen from the front garden, and one of the downstairs ladies (all of a certain refinement) could not forbear to remark: "Of course, you'll be getting new curtains." This may not have been the sole reason for tenseness between upper and lower premises, Blackacre and Whiteacre so to speak, for I remember making a grimace (very likely of the variety soon to be described) behind the windows of the foreshortened curtains, when one of the ladies was gazing up from the garden with what I took to be continuing criticism; conduct unbecoming a solicitor, particularly one with the nearby Equitable, and not utterly characteristic, though a fanciful recklessness when goaded must be accounted part of my personality.

What that personality was and became, its possessor would find uncongenial if not, in Marston's brother's phrase, insuperably difficult to depict in depth. Another result of the publication of *Souvenirs* was hearing after more than fifty years from a school friend, S. H. Birch, one of the "two pianists" referred to in the book. Birch's letters have abundantly confirmed my taste for puns, for playing the fool (eccentric dancing included) and for the grotesque, particularly in the domestic sphere. Needless to say, his jogging of my memory has confirmed my often being a simpleton in the affairs of life.

He proved to have been a great hoarder, and one of the school magazines he sent me records ("Old Boys' Notes") the departure from school of F. S. Shaw. Whether he went on to some other school before being articled to his solicitor-father, I do not know. He was a day-boy, with me in the fourth form when he left (and from the magazines I see now the highest form was the fifth, exiguous enough; there being no sixth). Though academically undistinguished, he was a sharpish fellow; light-brown hair brushed straight back, somewhat of a natty dresser. We were not particularly friendly, though conversing a fair amount on account of at one time sitting at adjoining desks. In one of his letters, Birch suggests that Frank Shaw was a secret smoker, and I think this was so; Birch rightly implying the habit to have significance. Apart from that, and what follows, his claim to memorability was his pulling of a face of unusual horribleness. I observed closely the steps required to imitate this, and have used them with success throughout life. The lower lip is held firmly by and behind the upper teeth; the eyes narrowed; and the upper cheeks inflated. Since this operation at its most effective involves holding the breath, the face increasingly reddens, the colour thus contradicting the general effect of a demented Chinese.

110

In the fourth form I had a Waterman fountain pen that disappeared suddenly. Did I suspect Frank Shaw? It may well be so, for I seem to recall him being previously involved in skulduggery. A fresh term arrived, perhaps another. Then I saw Frank Shaw quite openly using a Waterman. Through uncertainty and pusillanimity (the latter predominating), I did not challenge him at once; perhaps even surreptitiously tried the pen to make sure I was not mistaken — the nib had always been curiously scratchy, though suiting me in a way. "That's my pen," I said to him at length. "Is it?" he may well have simply said. Certainly he handed it over without demur, merely implying it had come into his hands in honest fashion (though the defence of such a case would have exercised the ingenuity even of his father's firm, one of renown in criminal matters). I heard of him, may even have come across him, during my own articles. He was finding it hard to pass the Law Society's examinations, no great surprise in the light of his performance at Seafolde House and premature escape from its ardours (and, I expect I thought, still linking worldly success with moral worth, in view of his illicitly acquiring my Waterman).

In my early days at Woolwich, defalcations by one of the Society's agents in Lancashire were discovered. The sum involved was not trivial and the Board decided to prosecute. This was precisely the kind of job Fred Shrimpton was glad to pass on to his recently-hired assistant. With the society's Internal Auditor, I went north to take evidence and lay the information with the magistrate's clerk. I must myself have prosecuted in the Police Court, where the agent was sent for trial to Quarter Sessions. In the latter place a member of the Bar would be required to represent the society. It was Fred Shrimpton's notion that it would be more efficient and convenient (it was still a novelty to me to have one well-to-do client — the Equitable — instead of a number usually unaffluent) to engage local solicitor agents to instruct Counsel (who would also be local) at the Quarter Sessions hearing. But it was my bright idea to employ Frank Shaw's father's firm, whose main office was not far from the Quarter Sessions town. I even knew the barrister I wanted, an able Junior remembered from my years in the north.

Part of the reference on the firm's letter of response consisted of familiar initials, and the firm-name was signed in a familiar hand, if not with the Waterman pen. At the sight of these things I felt a faint unease that apparently Frank Shaw was to be in charge, as though his attainments and character might not have evolved since

Fourth Form days. The possibility that he handled agency work, partaking as it did of the sharply coincidental, had never crossed my mind. Further and increased unease was in store for me a few days before the Quarter Sessions hearing: the news came from FSS that Counsel chosen by me was suddenly unavailable and the brief had been passed to Mr Howard Shaw. Only then did I recall what I had known since my articles, if not schooldays: that Frank Shaw had a brother at the Bar.

On the day of the hearing events went disconcertingly out of my control. Frank Shaw had changed little, though his cigarette-smoking had become overt, and his hideous face fallen into desuetude apparently. His lack of professional qualification was compensated for by a blasé familiarity with matters litigious, their mechanical side, like dealings with the Clerk of the Court, at any rate. The case against the agent was beyond doubt, but like most cases of embezzlement or fraudulent conversion needed care in presentation both to satisfy the technical requirements of the criminal law and strictly to prove a specific deficiency. The Assistant Secretary himself, Sandy Meikle, had travelled up with me and the Internal Auditor, to give evidence about the society's accounting system. Before the case was called, Frank Shaw's brother, and the defendant's Counsel, had got together and struck, not precisely what is known as a "plea bargain" but an understanding that the defendant would plead guilty if the prosecution soft-pedalled the heinousness of the crime. At this distance of time I am putting the thing crudely: exactly what Howard Shaw endorsed on his brief I cannot recall. At any rate, his exiguous presentation of the case opened the way to a plausible account by defence Counsel of misjudgement more than crime, and an expression of contrition. The defendant was merely bound over; the whole proceedings lasting no more than a few minutes.

Even at the time I realised I should have dug my toes in and prevented all this, awkward as it would have been — perhaps not possible. To say that Meikle, whose displeasure was always formidable, was unhappy at the one-sided quid pro quo would be doing the emotion an injustice. Probably he was also disappointed at not making an appearance in the witness box (the plea of guilty meant that no witnesses need be called), where his strong character and intellect, and mastery of figures and accounting procedures, would not have failed to impress. Perhaps in these more lenient times the idea of a chap "getting away with it", avoiding the punishment which might deter others minded to do the society down, would be widely thought desirable, but that was not a view I could then call in aid. Of course, matters of crime and litigation proved only a small part of my work, so professional deficiencies were rarely, if ever, revealed with such dramatic effect.

How conscious I am, even writing of the strange appearance of F. S. Shaw and my own discomfiture, that life at this epoch was too tame for autobiography, to say nothing of its insufficient distinction. J. C. Masterman, in his charming autobiography *On the Chariot Wheel*, makes the point that the flavour of a period may be misleadingly conveyed because memoirs are usually written by the distinguished or eccentric. I wish I could think I could add even a straw or two to the notion of the period covered. No doubt (though there is no such concatenation in my memory) as I anguished over Howard Shaw's perfidy, Hitler was denouncing the Polish Non-Aggression Treaty or the last shots were being loosed in the Spanish Civil War:

> All the posters on the walls
> All the leaflets in the streets
> Are mutilated, destroyed or run in rain . . .

Spender's lines, as so often in the Thirties, perfectly encapsulate a mood, a scene, but for those who had plighted their troth to a job, a family, a class, the tragic was always subservient to the comic. The mixture of genres could be more easily brought off in fiction than in the present attempt at what Walter Scott called vraisemblance. Besides, sixty years back, into one's childhood, memory's sieve is of so restrictive a mesh that whatever comes through seems to some extent worthwhile. But the memories of forty or so years ago start to jostle, an undistinguished crowd, and selection is more and more arbitrary.

When I think of Frank Shaw and the Waterman, I know that transaction took place in the fourth form classroom, at the extreme end of the school building (save only for the science lab added later), so that only one of the sliding wood-and-glass partitions bounded it when it was divided off after morning assembly. It was in this classroom particularly that was practised the curious craze of "fly-stunning" (as S. H. Birch recently referred to it in a letter, though I needed no real reminding). We became adepts at catching flies in the cupped hand. If a fly so caught was dashed, alive, to the ground, it was usually thereby stunned and could be crushed to death under one's shoe. Birch added, without assigning a reason, that he himself never participated in this blood-sport. He may have extended tenderness for living creatures to flies, as later I myself came to do, for like my other pianist school-friend, Birch was "good". I do not think S. W. Boldon was form-master throughout my entire stay in the fourth. Like a character in Jane Austen he left to marry and take Holy Orders; perhaps the last of the entirely orthodox masters. I suppose Mr Smith would have been his replacement; had come from some school in the tropics where waistcoats were superfluous — hence all his had been attacked by cockroaches while in drawers or suitcases. In England he wore them nonetheless. I worried about S. W. Boldon's discipline, cracked jokes about Mr Smith's hairy nostrils, in which his inserted thumb left plenty of room, but how short a temporal span separated such preoccupations from the "history" (to use Auden's catch-all word) the Thirties decade involved one in even against one's volition and everyday occupations!

To the Blackheath maisonette my mother came for a short time to convalesce after her partial thyroidectomy. The place was even less appealing to her than the Ashford flat: her ideas of suitable house property would have coincided with those of the Equitable. Internal doors and window-frames were painted dark green. We saw this as objectionable in the sitting-room at least, and bought some white paint. I made a start on the interior of the door but found it impossible to cover. Letting the paint down with turpentine never occurred to me, so well had cheap labour between the wars insulated even the modestly middle-class from what is now known as "Do It Yourself", and widely practised. We had to call in a decorator, but whether his ameliorations had been effected by the time of my mother's stay I forget. In any case, they were few, and there were plenty of other features to upset one whose attitude to such things was almost certainly stricter even than that of the downstairs ladies to curtains. When she was well enough to get up, and mount to the top floor, she discovered on the landing a disused sink (perhaps a relic of earlier days when that floor had been a separate flat) above a cupboard. The sink was more or less enclosed by timber, the whole affair painted in the formerly ubiquitous dark green. I had used the sink to store old magazines, probably mostly copies of *Left Review*. However, my mother's objection to this feature was grounded not in ideology but hygiene, no doubt allied to her strict conception of *comme it faut*.

114

There may have existed at this date what would also distress her — a moderately dilapidated car belonging to Jack Clark which by a stroke of ill fortune had one day broken down sufficiently near enough for Kate's help to be enlisted to steer it on to the premises, Jack being on his way to visit us. Who would have thought the car fated never to start again? Weeds and grass grew up in the shelter of its chassis, and in the end Jack had actually to pay to have it towed away to the junkyard. Luckily my mother did not experience the maisonette's fuel crisis in that first winter, when my son's pram had to be used to collect coal from the coal merchant, deliveries being held up. Nor am I sure she closely inspected the half of the back garden that belonged to us, the grass of which on one occasion was attacked by Kate with a pair of scissors.

My mother did, though, get upset in the ideological sphere. It was not long before even optimists saw Munich as merely slightly postponing the inevitable. During my mother's convalescent stay, or possibly somewhat later, my brother visited us. In a discussion about the future war both he and I said we would be conscientious objectors. She was horrified, left the room to shed a tear. The situation was exacerbated by a friend present expressing no such intent, though radical in politics. I can quite understand my mother's anticipation of family disgrace outweighing any wish for the odds against her sons surviving to be reduced. How serious my brother was I do not know: not at all, I should think.

> He only does it to annoy,
> Because he knows it teases.

The lines of the Duchess' lullaby would apply; the trait inherited by us from our grandfather — whom I see, as elsewhere described, rubbing his unshaven chin against my grandmother's cheek at breakfast time, and saying "diddle-diddle" in a loud falsetto. My brother was always appreciative, too, of abrasive conduct on the part of Mr Parslew, not at all rare. "Waiting, pleess!" had become a catch-phrase with us vis-à-vis any sort of delay or command, but as used and originated by Mr Parslew not always to be taken in a genial or lenient sense.

Part of my own expressed intent at that time of opting out of the coming war stemmed from the constant wish to shock, often noted by friends; a more serious part from the sense of the bogusness of the so-called National Government offering to resist fascist Ger-

115

many. Underlying all this, of course, was the lesson of the 1914–18 war — not to be bamboozled by imperialist motivations masquerading as national defence. But it was quite plain to me that conscientious objection was not legally tenable since I had never worked for pacifism in the moral or religious spheres, nor even expressed purely pacifist views.

As to such matters, why didn't I, in London's greater anonymity and opportunity, return to the political activity suspended during Ashford days? Easy to assign theoretical reasons, any of which may have really existed. I was no longer a simon-pure Stalinist, but did not accept the then anti-Stalinism, from whichever quarter it was expressed. Above all, I did not wish to see the former ruling-classes back in Russia. Some Marxist heresies had grown up among my Marxist orthodoxy, but there was probably no political party to which I could have given whole-hearted allegiance. To support inaction I might even then have advanced the feeble argument that a modern writer lives his politics in the act of writing, with all its difficulties of expression and audience — particularly if the writer concerned to a substantial degree sees life in political terms.

I should add, though, that politics did not come into a novel I wrote at this time, finished before the war, never published. It was inspired by a classic Scottish murder case where the victim took all night to die, in circumstances of some domestic complication and squalor. The notion was a reasonable one, for I also added a classic puzzle element, but the action being confined to one night, I proved to be still wound in Joycean or Woolfish coils, as described in *Souvenirs* — inescapably inside the protagonist's mind; scarcely admitting any gap in the hour by hour account of events. There was, however, an interlude when the hero mercifully dozed off, of surrealist nature and incorporating some features of my contemporaneous reading of Elizabethan and Jacobean dramatists. The latter was a brief salvation from the sin of unsystematic reading I have been guilty of throughout life.

My dubieties about the translation of Marxism into practical politics should not be exaggerated, as I realise apropos of what must have been my next fiction, *The Agents* — an episodic affair in the manner of Stevenson's *New Arabian Nights* or, more accurately, Arthur Machen's *Three Imposters*. The episodes were to be alternately true and false (achieved through varying narrators), the false motivated by a conspiracy for an English fascist *coup d'état*. Part of the conspiracy was a preliminary discrediting of the communist

116

left, and began with an episode that, when I described it to him, greatly appealed to Julian. The hero, wearing a Manx tweed suit, drawn by apparent chance into a communist meeting, is surprised to see so many women among the audience — women, moreover, all wearing mackintoshes, though highly made up. At a certain stroke of a nearby church clock, all the women stand, remove their mackintoshes, and reveal themselves as stark naked — implications, when the thing gets reported, of free love, wives held in community, and so forth, demonstrated practically at a communist rally. Or is there such a plot? The ambiguities were not to be resolved until the end of the book, when truth and falsehood would be identified and explained. However, the ideological sympathies would be no more in doubt than as in the case of a novel like Rex Warner's *The Wild Goose Chase*.

Warner's remarkable work had made quite an impression on me. It was published in 1937, but I see my own copy was not bought until June 1939 and probably re-read then. So it may, as well as Stevenson and Machen, have helped me to achieve the greater distancing and irony of *The Agents*. Certainly the writing indicated some literary progress, and the complicated, predominantly comic, plotting was worked out with ingenuity. Ben Jonson — that quintessentially English, though ever undervalued genius — also must have influenced plot and tone (though I pay tribute to him with due sense of inadequacy). And when I say English, I suppose I mean British, for as I write these words my bedside reading is Walter Scott's journal in which he sometimes quotes from Jonson, particularly from *Every Man in His Humour*, with almost proverbial effect. But though I started *The Agents* after the outbreak of war, I saw I could not go on with the thing after call-up (though opportunities would in fact have existed), for the activity seemed prospectively too irrelevant. Besides, history was rapidly undermining both plot and tone. (Amusing if somewhat macabre to think that nowadays the nude meeting might well be taken as a point not against but in favour of the left).

I mention these piddling literary matters not least as evidence of what progress can be made in matters of art by reflection and application; aiming at a sensible target. My follies in this field went on too long, considering my native wit; and insofar as they resulted from impulse and indolence, have gone on all my life. Of course, the distance between *The Agents* and one's actual involvement, outside one's volition, in the events of the war, was less than the distance of *The Wild Goose Chase* from such events (or so one would like to think). Rex Warner's novel, though the inspiration of its imaginative machinery lingered on, still holds to a romantic view of class character and destiny I believe I myself was growing out of, even at the time I was most involved in political activity. But such nuances are hard to recapture accurately. The last paragraph of *The Wild Goose Chase* may from the start have seemed too optimistic, for all that further ordeals were promised:

> The crossing of the marshes, the final battle with the king, birth in the desert and the strange customs of some remote tribes — of all this he thought then, and of all this we too have received strange and often self-contradictory information. Yet at this moment the light was clear and it was dead calm. Be the future as it might be, and no doubt that complete success was distant still, he knew that something not unworthy had been achieved already as he stood with the men and women, holding Joan's hand in his hand . . .

Hence the more lasting appeal of the boggarts and ironies and death-preoccupations in the verse of Graves and Riding and Norman Cameron.

8　The Strongroom

*War . . . extends the circle of one's acquaintance but beyond that
I cannot see that it has a single redeeming feature.*

— Raymond Asquith

I joined the Equitable on 1 December 1938. By 1 September of the
following year my wife and son had gone to Blackpool to escape the
metropolitan dangers of the war in which England became officially
involved on 3 September 1939. I have done little to suggest the
richness, for us, of what seems now an amazingly short span — a
mere gestatory period. It was a time of domestic happiness; of
greater comfort and prestige as a lawyer; and of modestly growing
literary know-how and friendships. (I see Ruthven Todd somehow
elevating himself behind the sitting-room door — still, appropriately,
in its dark green paint — to appear with black overcoat over his
head, arms in the sleeves: a vampire to gratify my small son's liking
to be reasonably frightened). Cutting across all theoretical political
desiderata was my wish (no doubt largely covert) that England
would rat again, as at Munich, so that peace should persist. This
feeling may have been partly rationalised but I doubt much inten-
sified by the belief, already touched on, that in a war against fascist
Germany England's participation would be half-hearted, alert for
the sell-out, the diverting of Hitler eastward, dirty work at the
crossroads generally. I guess my wish would have been the same
had England been led by the Archangel Michael.

Uniquely depressing, seeing my wife and son off at Euston; worse
for her, not least the retrogression of going back to her parents'
home. I have mentioned somewhere else the embarrassing shame
felt coming out of the house and seeing one's fellow men on the

morning the newspapers told of Germany's invasion of Poland, and it was apparent that general hostilities were inevitable. Strange emotion; of a kind a boy might feel seeing his parents arrive drunk on the school's sports day. It was probably on the evening of 1 September, after the office, I swam in the "lido" in Shooters Hill Road, thinking it could well be my last swim. It had been a hot summer: though the sky was overcast, the pool was warm, rather deserted. The sensation returns of swimming up and down, consciously luxuriating in my passage through the tepid medium, a passion even in the absence of war's sharpening.

I cannot recall when I dug the slit-trench in our part of the back garden, penetrating the scissors-trimmed turf. Grisly to have executed the work while my wife and son were still there. A slit-trench was said to be quite good protection against bombs. I do not know why I did not apply for an "Anderson" shelter. I think they were decried by the *Daily Worker* and other leftish voices scornful of the Government's A.R.P. plans. That would have sufficiently put me off.

Blackheath's pebble-rich soil, relic of the glaciation that scooped the Thames valley, resists the spade. I gave up the trench when it merely sheltered one in a recumbent posture. Now I come to think about it, my wife must have been there, for it was surely she who remarked that all I had done was dig a convenient grave. But in this hole I self-consciously went to lie for a few minutes on the Sunday morning when the sirens sounded after Neville Chamberlain's announcement that the country was at war. The sky remained clear.

Later that day I went to see Julian Symons at the Denmark Hill house he then shared with others. Herbert Mallalieu was there, or arrived there, his wife and child also self-evacuated. I accepted his invitation back to his flat in or near Croydon: probably neither of us relished that night alone in our family-denuded dwellings. In the middle of the night the sirens sounded again, wailing that like a chronic pain was to become familiar but never less disagreeable. Herbert and I dressed and went to a nearby public shelter and sat for some time, with a small but varied number of Croydonians, in semi-gloom, on benches against white-washed walls. No bombs fell, but we must have thought them likely to do, for when we returned to the flat before the "all clear" we stayed in the sitting-room, having hoisted a mattress against the window as a protection against flying glass, commonly identified as an air-raid hazard.

120

I was not due at the office on the Monday morning, which I expect inclined me to go with Herbert to Croydon. Austin Smith had issued instructions that in the event of war staff should allow three days to elapse, then report at certain assembly points. Like the rest of us, he was victim of the *Things to Come* complex. I let all Monday go idle and air-raidless by before phoning Mr Shrimpton and finding him and most staff already back at work.

The time that then had to elapse (taking in the Phoney War and Dunkirk and all that) before I was called up for National Service seems, in contrast to the pre-War period with the Equitable, curiously foreshortened. My wife came back to London for a few short visits, and I went up to Blackpool when I could, but for the most part I lived alone in the maisonette until the late autumn of 1940. I must have spent a lot of time at cinemas, and visiting Julian Symons at the Denmark Hill ménage brilliantly sketched in his *Notes From Another Country*. The essential misery of those days is indicated by the sparseness and confusions of the resulting memories. Call-up into the armed forces loomed vaguely but inevitably ahead. I registered with the twenty-eight years' old age group in the summer of 1940: another step to the grave. The scene was a large, mock-Tudor Eltham pub on a wide, bleak main road, appropriately Orwellian setting for the Orwellian smells emanating, during the medical examination part of the process, from men for the most part in what seemed to me amazingly advanced states of hairlessness, toothlessness and paunchiness. (Even fifteen or so years later, when my son registered for National Service, the medical officer, counting his teeth, arrived with surprise at the total of thirty-two). Being part of a sizable human mass was a strange experience: there were reminiscences of school and of my political past, but really little in life had been a preparation for so thorough-going an assault (however brief) on one's private individuality — as though caught for a crime of which one was not entirely innocent.

Mr Shrimpton, staff already depleted by the disappearance of Territorials and younger men, applied to the Law Society for the deferment of my call-up under a scheme administered by them. A few specious grounds were concocted to bring my case within the scope of the scheme (such as my work in the administration of arrears caused by borrowers' war service) but the application was rightly rejected. In the late Sixties, when I went regularly to the Law Society's Hall in Chancery Lane to sit on a working party concerned with conveyancing law reform, I saw again the little "court room", with its wealth of dark wood (more usually devoted to the appearance of wrong-doing solicitors before the Law Society's Disciplinary Committee), where the application had been heard; and the atmosphere of that war-time day — youth obsessed with time and destiny — came momentarily but sharply back.

Julian has also described, in the work referred to, how on the afternoon of 7 September 1940, a Saturday, he and I watched from the height of Brockwell Park, SE24, neat formations of German bombers, with attendant frisky-puppy fighters, moving overhead to raid the London docks. Soon, slanting cloud-mountains of smoke were seen rising from that area. This was more like *Things To Come*. The raid was renewed at night, which I was spending (or perhaps had decided to spend, in view of the cataclysm) at the house in Denmark Hill. We passed a few hours in a cellar: it seemed wise to do so, not having then acquired the half-devinatory, half-blasé sense of behaviour under such fire that soon came with more experience. When a bomb fell across the road on or close-by the University College Hospital, the coal in the cellar seemed to rise and re-settle itself, one phenomenon of the occasion that particularly struck me.

It must have been after the raids on London that Kate and I began regular (or, at any rate, previously arranged) evening telephone calls. Neither she in Blackpool nor I at the maisonette was on the 'phone. Did we ring a call-box number from a call-box? I certainly see myself in a call-box in Rochester Way in the early evening, and saying, in the course of a conversation: "There goes the siren. Can you hear it?" Lowering prospect for us both. On a few occasions, when the raid was especially bad and I was at home, I went to sit in the lower maisonette, where the three ladies would be, plus the fiancé of the daughter (a man of quite mature years), and possibly a neighbour or two. Hours of amazing tedium, scarcely alleviated by games of rummy, for love; modest refreshments. Any resentment about short curtains or Shavian horror faces had been forgotten or pasted over in the cameraderie induced by the raids. The ladies had even offered sleeping accommodation in a small room on the half-landing between ground-floor and basement, adjudged to be safer than our great bedroom on the first floor. I used it a bit, without necessarily taking in rummy or a cup of tea.

I saw much of Julian and his wife-to-be, who was none other than Kathleen, the middle Clark girl. They had come to know each other through us, of course; a consequence of my double life in

Ashford. Patiently they put up with a grass widower on the bum for meals and a bed and an interesting social life. I went often to the house in Denmark Hill and, when that became uninhabitable through an unexploded bomb in the garden, to a smaller house in Tierney Road, Streatham; the street memorable through the film star Gene Tierney (then a newcomer, later played the mysterious eponymous heroine of *Laura*), whose beauty I admired. With inexhaustible hospitality they never made me feel *de trop*. There was little on my part I could do for them, though long after the war was over they reminded me I had once dined them at Blackheath, making a hot-pot (culinary lore from Hollins Road days); and at Tierney Road cooked a meal of pork chops wearing my raincoat as protection from fat-splashes, rather as William Herbert Wallace was thought to have donned his before beating his wife to death with a poker.

A good many hours of that epoch of waiting for call-up were spent playing piquet and snooker with Julian, the latter in a convenient Temperance Billiards Hall. Apart from the few occasions provided by Councillor Marston's half-size table and some games in the basement of the Imperial Hotel with the pianist from the Metropole Hotel band, I was a newcomer to the latter game, but it is as much a tribute to Julian's skill as an indication of my novitiate that he used to give me no less than seven blacks. As the war advanced, that number may have been cut down to six. I love snooker, but have to put it in my life, really, in the rather large unvisited-Venice class of things.

I think Kathleen would rarely, if ever, come to the billiards hall; such places being as jealously masculine as Pall Mall clubs. I expect we would meet her if we were dining out. I say "dining", but the place that comes to mind in those purlieus is Bicards on the South Side of Clapham Common, one of a smallish chain of "caffs" of those days. A vision arises of the dark street, a few "exhalations whizzing in the air", pushing aside the black-out arrangement at the entrance, and moving into a not large, dazzling, crowded, smoky ambience, rather lower class than even the Joe Lyons emporia of the time. The safest dish on offer was baked beans on toast, but those with hardihood might order a pie.

Though slow, the tram became the most reliable way of getting between Woolwich and Streatham (the railway often upset by a bomb on the line or signalling system). I expect I am wrong but I think the journey involved only one change, at Victoria. I speak of

Woolwich rather than Blackheath because fairly soon that was always my starting point. One morning, in the early hours, I was wakened in the half-landing room by lumps of plaster falling on me in bed — or, more accurately, as I lay on the mattress I had lugged down from upstairs. I cried aloud: "Oh, no!" but without avail. A landmine had descended across the road, a little farther down: outside, in the dawn, were apocalyptic scenes.

With my usual reaction of making light of, even denying, personal disaster, I quite soon set about trying to clear up the chaos in our maisonette. Many of the heavy ceilings had been brought down and windows blown out. Nearly as bad as the ubiquitous plaster and glass was the soot sucked from the chimneys by the blast. I went on working past the start of office hours, and thoughtlessly failed to let the office know what had happened. One of the conveyancing managing clerks, R. J. Edwards, was sent or volunteered to discover my fate. After the war, he became the Solicitor's Department Manager, and I was lucky enough to inherit him as such when I succeeded Mr Shrimpton. He more than once told the story of that morning — approaching the house, increasing disorder, fire engines and A.R.P. personnel still evident, his car stopped, he proceeding on foot, the house with its windows out, no sign of life. Reg Edwards was convinced I was a goner, yet respectfully pressed the bell of the upper maisonette, though he could have walked in, the door having been blown off its hinges. To his astonishment he was greeted from the bathroom window-space directly above him by a grimy individual wearing a fishing-hat. No doubt his surprise was all the greater for his viewing me ordinarily in Manx tweed and the like.

I see now that putting on the hat was like my grandfather putting on eccentric hats when he went "golfing", as he called it: filling the scuttles with coal from the coal-place at 208 Hollins Road, Oldham. The business (described in my novel *The Perfect Fool*) had a rational basis — protection from cold and coal-dust — but my grandfather imposed elements of fantasy. The hat in question worn by me was one of a number of memorable possessions that disappeared during the war, not surviving the depredations of air-raid damage repairs men, furniture-removers, custodians of the furniture-store, and, I suppose, genuine accidental loss. I had bought it in some hatters' sale, not to go fishing in but because it closely resembled the hat worn by the model for Van Gogh's *Portrait of a Young Man*, the features of the young man himself very like my own, a fact that for some reason tickled my vanity.

Mr Edwards, a man of humour and practical ability, brought sanity into the situation. He was A.R.P. officer at Equitable House, and suggested I slept there for the time being: soberly considered, the maisonette was uninhabitable in its present plight. A couple of blankets and my overnight things were all that was needed to make the transition. With these, he drove me off, and I never went back to live in the maisonette. He must have been able to use his car still because of his A.R.P. role: I expect it was the pale green immaculate Singer he kept for a good few years after the War, having it resprayed black and cream during the vogue for two-tone bodies.

There was already a small, slightly shifting population of staff sleeping in the basement of Equitable House, in the strongroom where the deeds of the society's mortgage securities had formerly been kept, such deeds having been sent to premises near Westerham bought to house in safety the society's records and accounting organization. In the event, Equitable House was virtually untouched by enemy action: the deeds, stored in a tunnel in the chalk of the North Downs, suffered first from damp, then from an electrical fire caused by the drying machinery consequentially installed. A run of bundles in the "S"s (initial of the borrowers' surnames) were so badly damaged the titles had to be reconstituted, a task falling to the Solicitor's Department. By the time I returned to the office in 1946 the job had been done save for a hard core of cases resisting efforts to provide secondary evidence of legal ownership. These were passed to me, like some fiendish puzzle grown tedious. (Eventually, with the enlightened co-operation of the Land Registry, I cleared them all up).

As to the war-time race of strongroom dwellers, in some instances it seemed their stay was prompted or prolonged by a wish to escape — not only from quarters more vulnerable to bombs but also from the delays and dangers of commuting travel, even from wives and families. The mode of life offered by the strongroom (not for the last time the war had thrown up a Kafkaesque metaphor for existence), though constricted and monotonous, was not utterly unappealing compared with current alternatives. At the heart of it was a nightly nap "school", playing for small stakes but with proper seriousness, at the close of which orders were taken for fish and chips, volunteers not being lacking to brave blackout and bombs to journey to the nearby fish and chip shop. I more or less fell into this routine myself, though tempering time in the nap school with visits to the billiards saloon, also nearby, or a cinema.

The saloon, down an alley off Woolwich New Road, had been in peacetime a place of local disrepute, but I never saw anything untoward there. Freud noticed that obsessional people generally felt better in wartime, since the rest of the population had descended to their level: the former quarrelsome or larcenous frequenters of the saloon had no doubt found, or been drafted to, spheres of greater opportunity. The roof was of glass, so no one was much inclined to linger once the air-raid warning had sounded: it may well be that snooker did not in reality cut far into the evening's cards. A dim picture comes to me of my staying on in my room after office hours, engaged in some literary work, possibly *The Agents*, but I would have been no more steadfast in such a pursuit at that time than any other time of my life.

The description I have been giving of existence in the office and below it may well seem to indicate the nadir of my occupation as a lawyer, lower even than the bridge-playing and betting articled clerk days. When I was Oxford's Professor of Poetry, F. R. Leavis wrote to the *T.L.S.* calling my attention (about a point in one of my lectures) to a remark by A. N. Whitehead, saying justly but somewhat gratuitously that my "non-literary distinction" was "hardly comparable to that of the collaborator in *Principia Mathematica*." By then I was not utterly unknown in the solicitors' profession: what would Leavis have said had he wotted of me thirty years earlier? One can't help grinning at the business, but really the lack of distinction at the end of one's twenties in both prongs of the double life is no laughing matter.

In the evenings, in strongroom times, I sometimes went to the West End, perhaps fairly often, but memories of that, too, are not sharp. The atmosphere has often been described. The absence of lights, especially on moonlit nights, removed the city to earlier centuries. A measure of my continuing unsophistication about the literary world is that I was greatly impressed to sit, introduced by Julian or possibly Ruthven, at a table in the Café Royal with Bernard Spencer and his wife. Spencer, though he had not then published a book, was a poet I thought well of: a junior member of the Macspaunday group, had edited *Oxford Poetry 1930* with Stephen Spender. He was darkly handsome; his wife, Nora, pretty and chic, wearing one of the small felt hats fashionable at that time which fitted no part of the head. Though not formulating the matter in such terms, I was conscious that he was unlikely ever to be found in Bicards or round a halfpenny nap table. Nora died young, shattering for him, who never quite fulfilled his early promise.

In the strongroom, the most devout nap player was Arthur Pickup. Among the staff Fred Shrimpton had brought from the private firm formerly the Equitable's solicitors were two already elderly conveyancing clerks, rather a different breed from the bright secondary school boys recruited during the society's rapid expansion in the late Twenties. The two in question, Heap and Pickup, were apt to be named together, though not, I think, particular friends. Heap, whom I never knew well, had a nervous disposition, whereas Pickup, philosophically quiescent, seemed unmoved by outside events, even when bringing off, or falling down on, a nap call. Both stayed on after normal retirement age, had reluctantly in the end (after the war) to be asked to go, the one having become jittery, the other somnolent after lunch, neither of "good appearance and address", as I used to put it.

Forty years on, the figure of Pickup at the nap table is clear in my mind (as is his neat handwriting, his methodical way of undertaking a mortgage conveyancing case, established through many thousands having passed through his hands, his papers sometimes coming to me when some difficulty he reckoned beyond his powers, or, more like, what he was paid to carry the can for, arose). He rolled his own cigarettes, making them rather thin, keeping them between his lips as they smouldered away. Fairly frequently a cough would rearrange the liquescence in his lungs, rather as the bomb had rearranged the coal in the Denmark Hill cellar. His grey hair was thick, longish, greased, and parted more or less in the middle: Old Mother Riley without a bun may be envisaged. Deep lines ran from his nose in a colourless face. He had the trick, common in east and south-east London (and maybe elsewhere) of finishing off a remark with a rhetorical question, e.g.: "Well, I had to come back with another diamond, didn't I?"

Of less than medium height, away from the nap table he moved with modest pace on comfortably-fitting boots; outdoors wearing a large bowler-hat that came down low on his grey locks. He lived on the other side of the river: I think had been bombed out, in fact, but was probably unanxious to resume the daily journey in blitz conditions. What his wife was doing as a nap widow I do not recall, if I ever knew. Plainly he had the gift for hitting on the most comfortable existence possible, given an on the whole inimical world — which snowy and fluffy haired Heap had not.

Nor do I know the circumstances in which a young man called White appeared among the strongroom denizens. Though he was junior and very young indeed, I was aware of him as a staff member (in another department) before his strongroom life: perhaps he had brought me papers or a message; possibly I had noted his attitude or clothes, the latter running to sports jackets and flannel trousers when suits were *de rigueur* during the working day. Whatever the reason, he had not made a favourable impression: I discerned cockiness, potential argumentativeness if not actual impudence; or perhaps I merely took against him as a Dr Fell figure. One forms some sort of attitude towards every human, even those briefly encountered. In the discussions that went on in the strongroom while the cards were being dealt or fish and chips eaten, I soon found that White had communist views. We supported each other in questioning the Government's anti-fascist will and war aims; and, I expect, more unconvincingly, defended the role in the war of the Soviet Union, still to have its treaty of friendship with Germany made farcical by Hitler's invasion. But as to this last, impossible to say now how much one had been infected by the Trotskyist doctrines in the air at Denmark Hill and Tierney Road. By no means wholly on account of his ideas, thus revealed, it rapidly came to pass that I very much liked White — intelligent, straight-forward, untimorous. Being younger than I was, he was very soon called up: went in the R.A.F., became Sergeant, Air Crew, was killed. Such losses of the best never ceased to depress, all the more so following those of the Spanish Civil War — my friend Maurice Stott; that young man of infinite promise, Christopher Caudwell.

I must say something of myself as a poet at this period, conceited or self-important though the business may seem. One or two critics have noted that the outbreak of war had a firming effect on my verse: gave me "more to observe", Kenneth Allott remarked. I can't think I was aware of this at the time, though the start of my second book, *The Middle of a War* (1942), with a poem then called "November 1939" does sound a noticeably clear note, especially compared with what had mostly been going on in the Fortune Press *Poems*:

> Cigar-coloured bracken, the gloom between the trees,
> The straight wet by-pass through the shaven clover
> Smell of the war as if already these
>   Were salients or cover.

I remember the occasion of this poem. I was with Jack Clark on the Maidstone road, in the purlieus of Sidcup, the bourne, much later, of Harold Pinter's caretaker. We got out of a car he was driving (perhaps a forced alighting if the car was of the calibre of that previously left in our drive) and the scene at once seemed significant. Even in November, apparently, one's nerves were still sensitive about the changed state of the world.

Long after the war was over I came across an old file of typescript poems, and in the late Sixties and early Seventies revised some that seemed "capable of easy improvement by the removal of crudities resulting from lack of time and skill", as I put it in a note when some of the revised versions came out in *The Listener* in 1969. These *Listener* pieces, all post-war, were reprinted in *Tiny Tears* (1973). A few similarly revised poems, from the war years, were published as a pamphlet called *An Old War* in 1974 by Alan Anderson at the Tragara Press, Edinburgh. I am putting these latter poems in an appendix to this book, for they suggest the atmosphere and some preoccupations at various moments of the war years. But the work required to get them up to what I considered publishable level was often considerable, so it seemed the war had no general magical effect on my poetic prowess. I know poets mucking about with their past work usually do nothing but damage: here, however, poems pretty well beyond redemption had to be given salvation. Once more I feel that work on them was shirked at the time of original composition; even deceiving myself in 1969 by the phrase "lack of time".

All the same, the verse I wrote between the outbreak of war and my call-up is a better record of the world than what had gone before, not that that is claiming a great deal. The rhetoric is ballasted to some extent by observation and an occasional generalization of reasonable insight. But the sum total is meagre of those that revised or unrevised could be allowed to be seen by other eyes. The period covered was quite extensive in a sense, and even bombed out and benighted I welcomed the passage of the days as meaning fewer eventually in the disagreeable role of serviceman. No patriotic or even anti-fascist feeling tempered the urging on of time and the war while in moderate control of one's fate. Sometimes, moving well into 1941, a reassuring proportion of the months the war could last seemed already to have gone by; and then, considering German triumphs, British disasters, the weary laps ahead seemed unfairly numerous. There was still ample time in which to be scared, mutilated and killed. Herbert Read's poem of the First World War, "The End of a War", had given me the title for the sonnet I shall mention later, used also as the title of my second book. But I always had an uneasy sense of tempting providence by tagging 1942 as the middle of the business. That might prove to be an early year, the duration of the First War no criterion at all for the length of this.

I must have got my "papers" at the beginning of April 1941. I had to report on the 21st. I cleared up at the office so as to spend the interim with my wife and son in Blackpool, aiming to go straight from there to report. How did I get my blankets from the strongroom back to the maisonette? Or was our furniture already in store and the maisonette boarded up? Was I conscious of my last game of nap, thinking it rather more ultimate than my supposedly last swim? The questions are sufficiently banal, the answers probably only too boringly recoverable from my letters of the time. Fiction would have invented a livelier circumstantial narrative.

9 The Andrew

The bachelor 'e fights for one
  As joyful as can be;
But the married man don't call it fun,
  Because 'e fights for three—
For 'Im an' 'Er an' It
  (An' Two an' One make three)
'E wants to finish 'is little bit,
  An' 'e wants to go 'ome to 'is tea!

—Kipling

Andrew . . . The Royal Navy — O.E.D. (supp.)

When I was a small boy, perhaps seven, on holiday in Blackpool, I was taken to a show called "The Battle of Zeebrugge". This was held near the place where a dozen or so years later (staggeringly short time for the change in *moeurs* and my own persona) the Reverend Harold Davidson sojourned in a barrel. Entry being proposed by my father, I keenly looked forward to the proceedings, always eager to be entertained. What confronted the audience was a small stage, such as puppets perform on, with a single set throughout — the famous Mole, which even I had heard of, captured during the recently-ended First World War by the Royal Navy (plus, presumably, the service in which Richard Flower served with such distinction) against murderous fire from the German defenders. The thing was within an ace of being a fiasco, but in the end went down as a triumph of British seamanship and arms. On Blackpool promenade, the depiction of this affair was effected by model ships (worked from below the stage) sliding up to the Mole, some doubtless sliding back, or disappearing beneath the cardboard waves. Flashes

131

from the guns on both ships and land were ingeniously arranged, the sound of the explosions pretty well continuous and ear-splitting. I was terrified, may have cried and had to be taken out, though the impression remains that much was endured.

I continued not to like loud bangs. A firearm produced on the stage even by a comic, put me on tenterhooks until the thing was let off or put away. Chekhov's dictum that if a pistol is imported into theatrical proceedings it should sooner or later be let off was too often adhered to for my liking. In later years, caring slightly less what people thought of me, I sometimes put my fingers in my ears during the suspensive period.

I told in *Souvenirs* of my apprehension as a youth, when embarking on "Uncle" Fred's yacht, that he might command a voyage beyond the calm confines of the Ribble estuary: indeed, even there I would keep a weather eye on the water ahead for signs of "white horses" always glad when Mr Marple turned the wheel to head the vessel away from the open sea. Once, on holiday in Llandudno, my mother had engaged a rowing boat to take us out fishing, probably at my brother's urging, even mine (for children do not always obey their instincts). The experience was disagreeable, cut short; perhaps the origin of my fear of waves, nausea at the smell of stale fish — often seemingly detectable in boats unconnected with piscine activity, usually mingled with the odours of oil and what one imagines to be bilge. Later experiences of the sea were confined to voyages to the Isle of Man, to France once, and to Jersey for our honeymoon: none traumatic but not lessening the sense of Thalassa's power to discomfort, even kill.

In view of all this, why when registering for call-up did I express a preference to serve in the Royal Navy? The sensible thing, as many unbrave realised at the time, would have been to opt for ground duties with the R.A.F. But in pre-call-up ignorance one wondered if one wouldn't be whisked into the air against one's option, and I feared heights more than the sea (not to mention the dangers of aerial combat). In any case, to go into the R.A.F. with the proviso that one wouldn't fly seemed a contradiction in terms somewhat insane as well as infra dig. (Later, eventually getting by chance into the Fleet Air Arm, a similar guilty sense arose, though in that service there was a reassuring apophthegm: "only fools and birds fly".)

The over-riding motivation for my choice of service was certainly the memory of the horrors of 1914–18 trench warfare, perhaps got

132

almost first-hand from such as Issy Gotliffe, undoubtedly revived by the grisly war fiction suddenly popular in the late Twenties. Who could be sure such monstrous conditions would not come again? Besides, if killing and being killed were in question it seemed better for this to be done at a good distance — and here, rather than those of Zeebrugge, the memories of the Battle of Jutland played a part. My surviving brother had been born on the day of that naval action, so it had always interested me. The distance between the rival fleets had been almost reassuringly great. Finally, Rex (I will retain the name Julian gave him in *Notes From Another Country*), of the Denmark Hill ménage, had had no doubt at all that he would put in for the Navy. He said it was the superior as well as the senior service. Why one should have been impressed by the view of an unemployed Trotskyist activist in this realm of knowledge is not now easy to understand, especially as one surmised that Rex's overmastering reason for his preference was that in the Navy he would be able to keep his beard, as blonde and virile as Gumbril's false one in *Antic Hay*, and, as an appendage of youth, nothing like as commonplace then as today. As a matter of fact he had initially to shave it off (for whiskers may be worn in the Navy only if grown with permission), and appeared on his first leave with the near-unrecognizable, weak-chinned look later to be noted as common to all the suddenly beard-shorn, whether opisthognathous or not.

On the morning of the day I had to report, my wife came to Blackpool Central Station to see me off. Leave-taking was rendered low-key by our encountering Gilbert Waller, also making for the London train. I imagine his history of tuberculosis, despite the abiding success of the UMKALOBO treatment, had given him a medical category that exempted him from call-up, though he could already have been London correspondent for the American newspaper which might well have reserved him anyway and certainly at a later date put him into U.S. army officer's uniform — olive drabs, was it called? — as a war correspondent, transmogrification impossible to accept with a generous spirit or straight face. He had probably been visiting his parents in Blackpool.

We had a third-class (as it then was) compartment to ourselves. He had learnt of the reason for my journey with the interest and underlying glee of the journalist encountering the unusual, probably tinged with *Schadenfreude*. He was in no doubt the occasion must be marked with a bottle, and went off up the train to arrange it. At mid-morning (barely that), in mid-war (whatever scruples one might soon have about titling a book of verse), success seemed unlikely. That would have suited me, whose low spirits were not alterable with alcohol: besides, one did not want to go back to days of sneezing powder and like japes, as booze in such circumstances threatened to indicate. However, Waller fairly soon returned with nose twitching and lips pursed more than usual, not long after followed by a steward and a bottle of claret and two glasses. Waller paid with complacency the six shillings or so demanded, taking the money from a purse of the kind he always used — the stiff opening flap held horizontal and a few coins urged into it (for easy extraction) with a slight motion of the wrist.

I seem to think that on arrival at Euston he persuaded me to go to Charley's café in Marchmont Street. Did he have a golden pudding and a cup of tea? Was the pin-table still there and did we play it? Such things savour of fiction, yet may well have occurred. I was already a good way from the character I had presented in London in the early Thirties, yet much remained of the Gissingesque concern for others that would have kept me to a degree in Waller's thrall.

However the interim was occupied, it must have been late afternoon, more likely early evening, before I was in the train leaving Liverpool Street Station for Harwich. I had to report to a training establishment called H.M.S. *Ganges*. Possibly the train's departure was delayed: certainly there were many hold-ups on the journey itself because of heavy air-raids. Could one read on the train? I think so: it was only the blindless suburban and local rolling-stock where the sole illumination was a dim, blue, aquarium-like light. Nevertheless, as the train jerked on, one tired of or exhausted one's reading-matter, and sat in excruciating boredom, occasionally squinting past the sides of the blinds at the flat landscape lit fitfully by flashes from anti-aircraft guns. Perhaps, indeed, the lights had been lowered because of the raids. More and more passengers alighted as the various Essex stations were reached until, like the voyagers in Sutton Vane's play *Outward Bound*, who gradually realise they are all dead, one saw preponderantly remaining men of a like age to oneself, obviously en route for *Ganges* — a destination seeming almost as remote as the sacred river itself. Two or three of us got together, compared notes. I was glad of this, my anal-erotic character having made me anxious and guilty about the growing certainty of arriving later than the time specified.

134

H.M.S. *Ganges* was at Shotley, opposite Harwich on the Orwell-Stour estuary. While there I usually went "ashore" to Ipswich, so Harwich remained largely unknown. That dark night of arrival it was utterly mysterious, not much of it traversed: the train drew up at the harbour and we were soon picked out by someone in authority, perhaps a petty officer, as *Ganges* fodder, and led to the quayside. I have sometimes fancied we were rowed over to Shotley, but I think that is to be too much at the mercy of the Styx parallel: a small ferry boat was probably involved. There was room for the newcomers to be tinctured by naval personnel returning from a night "ashore", their insobriety assorting ill with the prevailing mood.

On the far side of the gloomy river the black-out made *Ganges* equally mysterious: of the initial process of induction all that remains clear is of a petty officer taking a few of us into a galley and offering cocoa, apologising that it was too late for supper. Though a piece of bread-and-butter may have been also offered. The cocoa was a left-over, tepid, very thick, drawn by the P.O. with a long-handled ladle from the bottom of a metal vat. Later, the beverage became familiar, the solid chocolate slabs from which it was made sometimes available, through bribery or pilfering, for eating. The shining cleanliness of vat and ladle — indeed, of the whole galley — impressed me much, as it would have even my mother. Also impressive was the service given by the P.O., which I soon realised was characteristic of the R.N. — a rough affection, manifested in countless ways; touching really. The incident may well have taken my mind back to supper times at Seafolde House, though the "coker" brought by the maid there was a vastly inferior brew.

Eventually, one found oneself in a dormitory, also reminiscent of Seafolde House, though much larger than any sleeping accomodation supplied by the Boss. Crowning the fictional coincidences of the day, in the next bed, or preparing to get in it, was a man called Rod Davies, a colleague of my wife's when before marriage she had worked for the *West Lancashire Evening Gazette*. I had known Rod quite well in those Blackpool days of half a dozen years before — solid, fresh-faced, competent, unflappable. He had then been a reporter; since become editor of a local newspaper elsewhere. Immediately the populous setting and, as in a dream, one's getting undressed in the midst of it, seemed somewhat less bizarre.

In my first letters from H.M.S. *Ganges* I described it as resembling a bad boarding-school, but this was not accurate. Truer to say it was like an exceptionally good boarding-school, certainly of the Thirties. Many of the facilities — billiards tables, cricket tables, gymnasium, and so forth — were first-class, and the food was abundant, excellent in its way. The Boss would have been staggered at the size of the helpings. As previously mentioned, each mess drew its food from the central galley, and (to take an example) the portion of "figgy duff" (generic term for a pudding the staple of which at *Ganges* was a baked sultana cake) allowed for each man was the dimensions of a half-brick or near them. I was already affected by the dyspepsia later to become a nuisance. It disappeared under the *Ganges* régime of extreme physical effort and low-level mental concerns, and I was not over-faced by the half-bricks, though in early days had a bilious attack through eating a double portion of corned beef, a deadly dish even in moderation. Uniquely at *Ganges*, in all my life, I was conscious of physical fitness; and that sense seemed to make it natural to go along with *Ganges* pursuits — squad drill, P.T., swimming, gymnastics, a violent species of football played with a soccer ball one was allowed to handle — most of which would have otherwise struck a non-games-playing solicitor in his thirtieth year as preposterous.

Ganges had been the training establishment for boy entrants to the Navy, only as a result of the war used for initial training courses for "Hostilities Only" ratings. The school parallel certainly applied to its division into "Annexe" and "Main Camp". Each batch of entrants spent a week in the Annexe, getting kitted-up, injected, instructed in the arts of donning uniform, saluting, and recognizing rank, and suchlike; and then five weeks in the Main Camp. One of the surprises in the school magazines sent to me by Birch after the publication of *Souvenirs* was the reminder that Seafolde House had a topographically separate "Preparatory School": its function and *mores* were, I imagine (I was too old for it when I joined Seafolde House), not unlike those of the *Ganges* Annexe. Incidentally, I learnt from one of the magazines that in the Preparatory School sports of 1926 the Mothers' Race was won by Mrs Sage. She probably had proportionately longer legs than her diminutive son, for carrying whom (after he had graduated to the senior school) my brother was once beaten by the Boss, as related in *Souvenirs*. Sage and others (even those of more normal stature), when at the Preparatory School, under the benevolent dispensation of two women teachers, must have heard with a degree of awe and terror of what they would have to face when they went to Seafolde House itself. So it was, *mutatis mutandis*, for those in the Annexe vis-à-vis the Main Camp, arduous routines and demon N.C.O.s said to be special menaces, and I daresay more specific threats now gone from recall. What could never be forgotten was the 143 feet high mast, which authoritative rumour had it must be ascended by one and all before "passing out", some question remaining whether the short vertical ladder at the top was comprised in the task. I put this prospect out of mind, not alone in saying that after all one couldn't be forced up the thing.

I suppose another school parallel was the desire to conform, even excel, despite distaste for some of the pressures involved; the feeling not excluding the frequent assertion of one's personality to those in authority. I could write at length about the problems arising over uniform, and slops generally, usually a blend of the communal and the individualistic, but equal interest from others could scarcely be expected. Some points must be made, however. There was a conflict between my thriftiness and my wish to be, in the word of my Blackpool tailor of old, as "tony" as possible. On registration I had been accepted by the Navy as a Writer (the instant conferring of such status, compared with my still unfulfilled yearning to be a writer, an irony not lost on me at the time), but subsequently being over-stocked with Writers they called me up as an Ordinary Seaman, so I was issued with "square rig" uniform. One received two sets of blue serge jumper and trousers, best and every day, "Number Ones" and "Number Twos". In my case the jumper of the latter was rather too loose about the hips, but I never took it to a jobbing tailor to have it taken in. Though quite satisfied with my Number Ones, I realised that to the discriminating eye one would always look a sprog in them. It was possible to have the jumper's neck-opening and the trousers' bell-bottoms enlarged, the result being, if longer tapes were substituted on the jumper, a passable imitation of the bespoke "tiddly suit" possessed by many, perhaps all, regular R.N. matelots. I did not take this step, held back as much by modesty at lack of active service as parsimony. There was also the sense that the resultant outfit would be bogus after all. A fellow recruit called Flitcroft, a schoolmaster, revealed unsuspected adaptability to proletarian marine form by appearing in the slightly outré bespoke version of Number Ones while still at *Ganges*.

A session was devoted to instruction by a P.O. on how to put on square rig — strange, on the whole becoming, guise; as historically determined but probably more complicated than any sacerdotal garb. Over a vest, if one wore one (and vests were an issue), went the "cotton 'flannel' " — the two sets of inverted commas needed to delineate the garment itself and its derivation from a like garment made in former days of flannel, not cotton. A. Cecil Hampshire in his *Just an Old Navy Custom* describes the cotton flannel as a precursor of the T-shirt: good point, the thing being short-sleeved and of less than normal shirt length. It was square-necked, however, and thus liable to reveal the shoulder straps of a vest (if worn), as in the case of an unsmart female. On top of the cotton flannel went a blue, white-braided collar, secured by an arrangement of tapes, fastening round the waist. The collar had to be put on before the trousers, which were kept up with a broad, blue, adjustable webbing belt that was fastened before the flap at the front of the trousers was lifted and buttoned — no flies on matelots. The jumper could only be donned by first putting one's arms right into the sleeves (the buttons at the cuffs undone), then manoeuvring the head into the buttonless neck-opening. After the jumper had been persuaded down over the hips, the previously-secured, separate collar had to be pulled out and made to lie over the similarly-shaped serge collar of the jumper. A black "silk", folded narrowly, was then passed under both collars, the ends put together, folded under, and tied down with two blue tapes at the V-opening of the neck of the jumper. A white lanyard was worn only on posh occasions. It should be added that in winter a long sleeved jersey went over the cotton flannel and under the jumper; and that off-duty the separate collar could be untied and slipped off. As to the latter, as I write the words the vision comes pat — not vouchsafed to the outer world — of men collared only by their navy-blue jumpers, drinking pints in the N.A.A.F.I., writing letters, and (in establishments like the R.N.A.S., Lee-on-the-Solent) carrying their enamel mugs and "irons" (knife, fork and spoon) to supper.

On kitting-up, there were no trousers matching the jumper of my Number Twos to fit me. In his book *The Prof*, Roy Harrod said that working for Lindemann's "S Branch" he discovered early in 1941 that twenty million pairs of trousers had been produced for an army consisting at that time of only two million men, so that may well have caused a naval shortage. For several days I went about (not alone in my incongruity, for a number of giants and midgets were in similar case) wearing the grey flannel trousers in which I had crossed Lethe's river — under cap and jumper, over pusser's boots. Like Widmerpool's overcoat, the embarrassing trousers marked one off from most of one's fellows (again a reminiscence of boyhood emotion): pleasure and relief came with the delivery of more trousers to the clothing store, and one felt oneself repaired.

Further to the healing business, the question arises how soon I felt that joining the Navy had ended my "divided life". I use the unoriginal, not awfully descriptive phrase to indicate the condition of intellectuals' souls referred to by Matthew Arnold (to go no farther back), and the various alienations of bourgeois existence specified by Marxists. It could not be said that suddenly one's heart was in one's work, unlike being a solicitor; yet since no choice, no possibility of abdicating, existed, there was scarcely a wound that called for being sutured. As a rating, one was pretty effectively proletarianized, even though better off than most (for the Equitable made up my salary). And the business of being a writer, yet with an audience measured merely in hundreds — which so many Thirties writers saw as ludicrous and longed to break out of without compromising their art — seemed to me then likely to be ended as the experience of ordinary mankind became my own experience, and the feeling quickly grew that I wouldn't, as Wilfred Owen had succinctly put it, "want to write anything to which a soldier would say No Compris." What has been referred to before, the sense that with the coming of the war nothing would ever be the same again, was made more plausible, more precise, by the experience of service life, certainly in its earlier stages. Not that in the first weeks at *Ganges* the question of writing verse arose. Events were better suited to prose, but I didn't write that either, not even to the extent of keeping a journal.

At the end of the Annexe week, volunteers were requested to make up a small party to stay a second week in the Annexe to help the permanent staff with the next batch of recruits. I volunteered, a barrack stanchion in the making. It seemed a wholly non-disadvantageous way of spending yet another week away from the sharp end of war. It was at a peaceful Sunday supper when my own entry had left for the Main Camp and the new had not yet arrived, and leisure and rations were ample, that I over-ate at the sulphuretted hydrogen-producing corned beef. I must have recovered by the next day, for I remember walking purposefully over the Annexe's modest parade ground in view of the new recruits straggling in with their suitcases, thinking they would imagine me an old sweat despite the loose-hipped jumper — as a boy with one term's experience displays himself to new boys. A good job my Number Twos trousers had by then arrived.

When I moved over to the Main Camp I found myself made Class Leader — a sort of temporary local Leading Hand. We (a class of Ordinary Seamen) shared a mess with a class of Writers, their Class Leader being a Writer to the Signet called Milne, whose Scots conscientiousness and efficiency made up for my own deficiencies as a leader of men. At the end of the course I asked the senior of the two N.C.O.s in charge of the classes why he had chosen me as Class Leader. He said he always chose solicitors, if available; one of few laymen with a good opinion of the profession. Just inside the entrance to the mess was a tiny room containing brooms and cleaning material and the like, but also a table and chair for the use of the Class Leaders in the disposal of such slight paper-work as came their way, and perhaps regarded as a privilege in return for extra responsibilities. It was there I wrote my first poem after joining the Andrew, "ABC of a Naval Trainee". Julian Symons, not yet called up, was editing an anthology of war poetry for Penguin Books and asked me for a poem, so the piece was written to order, in a stanza based on that of the "Epilogue" to Auden's *The Orators*, itself based on a traditional poem. The anthology project (and the excellent way it was fulfilled) was an indication of Julian's coming status as a man of letters of remarkable range, accomplishment, and clarity of mind: for me, it was a chance not to be missed to appear, in however small a way, before a wider public.

I don't believe I finished any other poem at *Ganges*; not even attempting more than two or three. Why the poetic drive should have been so weak in one enjoying robust health, amid fresh scenes, is difficult now to explain (beyond a general charge of poetastry). Some years ago, in a minute, unfilled notebook of the time, I found a few lines whose subject seemed promising, about the old ship's figureheads that stood at the edge of the huge parade ground of the Main Camp, by the dread mast. These garishly painted images — bearded gods, high-breasted nymphs, staring-eyed young mariners — might surely have been worked up into emblems of one's then present plight, and future traffic with the sea. But probably my mind was still too ideologically rigid for poetic fancy so to function. And as to the non-apocalyptic side of things, somehow I did not see until some months later that what I wanted — was able — to say about my changed life could be done in quite a simple way.

The cupboard-like room was also where I skulked on Sunday mornings, having been told by some mildly exasperated and baffled officer to keep out of sight at such times. This arose through my having said, when asked to state my religion on joining *Ganges*, that I was an atheist, as happened to be so. The Regulating Petty Officer (or whatever he was, ignorance prevailing in such areas at that juncture) had initially baulked at putting this down, but I provided no alternative and was possibly persuasive in the forensic style valued by the Class Leader-choosing Chief. What a mistake! I have a feeling Rex told me that on joining the Navy he had put himself in the godless category, but I wonder how official the business was in his case. Being classified as "Atheist" almost always caused trouble, starting with that R.P.O. and immediately continuing with the fellow at the Annexe who stamped identity discs with name, rank, number and religion. There was room only for a few letters to indicate the last-named, so, after some discussion, my disc read "ATH", which would surely have baffled any R.N. burial party had the occasion arose, perhaps causing a fruitless search for the funerary ceremonies of, say, some sect calling itself after Athanasius. When I was on a course in Aberdeen, I was told to march the Church of England party to and from the church (or cathedral, as perhaps it was), leaving an awkward hour or so to fill in — the office plainly designed as a punishment on earth for my irreligion. On a few later occasions I feigned to be C of E to avoid any such chores, to say nothing of acrimonious arguments, and when eventually commissioned allowed myself to suffer a nominal conversion (or, rather, return) to that belief.

Almost as mysterious as the gift of religious faith was the acquisition in the Navy of the status of C.W. Candidate; that is to say, someone who after suitable and successful novitiate service would be put on a course leading to a commission. That I was such a Candidate was intimated to me during training by the Divisional Officer, my spiritual deficiencies apparently no bar. For such Candidates initial training was followed by drafting to a capital ship, and I did not doubt that that would be my next step, reassured rather than otherwise that I should be facing sea and enemy in something of substantial dimensions and armament. But towards the end of my time in *Ganges* a notice appeared outside the Divisional Office inviting volunteers for a course, qualification being School Certificate credits in Mathematics and Physics. The notice was otherwise inexplicit, but a "buzz" went round that a spell at a civilian technical college was involved. The implied amplitude of the thing, to say nothing of the postponement of big ship service, greatly appealed — a superior version of the extra week at the Annexe. Thanks to the demonic teaching of the Boss, I was more than qualified on the Mathematics side, and though I had dropped Physics in favour of Chemistry for Matriculation, I must have had it at School Certificate level, for I was accepted for the course. The Divisional Officer thought it ill-advised to defer or obfuscate normal progress towards an executive commission, but I paid no heed to him, and not until time had removed war's perils safely into the past did I come to think with a tinge of regret that I might have had a more satisfactory and less boring war, if a shorter life, had I let my name be struck off the list. Its going forward (with others I knew) for the unknown training (said to be to do with wireless telegraphy) made no difference to matters at *Ganges*.

The weather on the Suffolk coast had started that April with a wind from the steppes, adding to the discomforts of the much-frequented parade ground. Only belatedly did it become milder, eventually hot; and in my last week an exotic number appeared in Orders of the Day specifying the rig, which being interpreted proved to consist of cotton flannel and white duck trousers. By then, the class' skill at squad-drill was remarkable, only marred by the ineptitude of one member, a gentle effeminate individual who simply lacked physical co-ordination. When we graduated to rifle-drill a fresh P.O. took over, small and combative, reputation long preceding his actual appearance (though he was nothing of a bully and sometimes inadvertently revealed a kind heart). He once exasperatedly cried out to our awkward member, using a noun seemingly rising unbidden to his lips, for I never heard him use it before or after: "You — you — you cream-puff." Possibly the hesitation was occasioned by his feeling the need to temper in some way the second part of the compound, which would accord with his inner tenderness. It was the same P.O. who, chiding the class for clumsiness in returning bayonet to scabbard, said of the latter: "You'd find it all right if it had hair round it" — but this was plainly premeditated, probably of ancient lineage.

Despite what is generally held to the contrary, and no doubt except for our cream-puff, we came to enjoy squad-drill. Since the class had originally been categorized as one of Writers, all its members were middle-class (using the term to cover some such spectrum as local government clerk to chartered accountant), mainly the same kind of secondary school boys on whose foundation the Equitable's expansion had been grounded, so puritanical work-ethic in various aspects would play its part. As Class Leader I was *ipso facto* "corporal" of the "Colour Guard", a small squad selected to perform an elaborate manoeuvre at (I think) the last Sunday morning "divisions" the class would attend before leaving. The Navy is good at drill, as may be seen by direct comparison when it takes part in ceremonies jointly with other services. I have no compunction about boasting that my Colour Guard did not disgrace the tradition. Similar considerations applied to the gymnasium, where quite soon the instructor was introducing the class to challenging, and thus interesting, skills. It was like the episode in the Paul Newman film *Cool Hand Luke*, where the convict chain-gang suddenly find corporate identity and finish a day's road-tarring with two hours to spare. Also it somehow accorded with the notion, still held, that a common effort could productively outdo individual enterprise.

But too bland a picture must not be presented. Usually in the gymnasium — occasionally to be seen throwing off a few press-ups, or evolutions on the parallel bars — was a short figure in white sweater and flannels. One had seen him about the gymnasium purlieus wearing over this garb a naval officer's cap and jacket. His rank was Sub-lieutenant, R.N.V.R., his age a good deal less than mine. In his own eyes he was ruler of the gymnasium (though some superior officer with that responsibility must have existed), not averse to ticking off all and sundry whether challenging his territory or not. It had to be admitted that this chap must by definition have done some big ship service, but it irked me to see him, with his cocky character and pocket Hercules appearance, lording it safely in *Ganges*, building up his already excessive muscle.

The two N.C.O.s in charge of the class have already been mentioned. Both were time-expired men, called back in consequence of the war. The elder, a Chief Petty Officer, big, grey hair, ruddy features, a rather squashed Roman nose like Sir Frank Benson's, had been a deep-sea diver, full of stories of that occupation. He it was who had faith in lawyers. The younger, a Petty Officer, more intelligent in a general way, had gone into the Borstal service after serving his time. When Borstal officers are criticised I always think of him — so quiet, authoritative, lucid, and concerned for those in his charge. He gave me an abiding soft spot for Borstal officers, as did its wartime services for the Salvation Army, often to be found

143

where other amenities were absent. The P.O.'s instructional lectures or talks were particularly good, undeserving of the sleep that fell on many at the theoretical ones, where we were sitting down. Nights were apt to be disturbed, for if the air-raid warning sounded everyone had to get up. As Class Leader I was saved from having to go to the shelters; being on duty in and just outside the mess, on guard for incendiaries, perhaps parachutists. What torture, the business of waking to the siren and putting on trousers and sweater (gaiters excused), after a day of intense physical activity and likely an evening of N.A.A.F.I. beer. Almost equal torture trying to keep awake during a talk on, say, the Rules Concerning Lights at sea — though that was a topic less soporific to me than most, since some of its precepts had been reduced to verse, starting in near-metaphysical style:

> When both Lights you see ahead,
> Starboard wheel and show your Red.

"Wondrous heavy" — Gonzalo's phrase for the magic slumber overcoming him on Prospero's island would rise to mind as I sat on a back-row bench after a half-brick portion of figgy duff.

Being Class Leader also saved me from many menial duties, though I had had a fair share of these in the Annexe, including Captaincy of the Heads. The protected life-style before 1939 of even the modestly middle-class male is demonstrated by the recollection that when in the Andrew I initially had to use a broom I simply imitated the grasp and motions I had seen others use (perhaps most closely observed in childhood), rather surprised at their efficaciousness in directing the broom's function. It was the same with darning and ironing, the former possibly now a dying art in days of ubiquitous man-made yarns. As to the latter, I actually sent the bulk of my washing home from *Ganges* (and perhaps later places), but one was always washing and ironing one's square rig collars, in the hope of paling the obdurate navy-blue, tell-tale of a recent recruit. (A few bought collars — not from pusser's stores — actually made in pale blue, but these were easily detectable and merely demonstrated the narcissistic duplicity of their wearers). The lessons learnt at *Ganges* were a bizarre mix of the bellicose and the domestic; in that, imitating life, certainly during many periods of history, admittedly mostly primitive. Perhaps the domestic arts were emphasised through the routines remaining, quite a few, of the former boys' establishment. Our class N.C.O.s encouraged us to whip round (or did a modest mess fund for such purposes exist from the start?) to buy a supply of Red Cardinal polish (thereafter kept, I suppose, in the Class Leader's poetry-writing cubby-hole) to incarnadine the stone flags on which stood the cylindrical iron stoves that heated the mess. For weekly Captain's rounds, the mess-tins and so forth were burnished and laid out in prescribed order, as at the foot of each man's bed was his considerable kit, and empty kit-bag, the latter presented so as to display its base, on which his name and number had been painted in black at the elaborate and prolonged kit-marking routine in the Annexe (during which, as has been sufficiently said, I was tagged "ATH", which did not excuse me, however, from the hieretical laying-out ceremony).

Were we conscious of the strong lingering force of tradition in all this, the rough, by and large triumphant, tradition of British naval history, of the ascerbities and moral standards of the Empire — traditions made fugitive, not to say despised, in the minds of those radicalised by the two decades between the wars? Looking back, the kit-marking routine, the kit itself, seems evidence at once of England's greatness and archaism. I single out almost at random, among that considerable issue of *matèriel*, the substantial japanned tin box for caps; the excellent shoe and clothes brushes, still in good order after forty years; and the dolly-bag made of stout, unbleached linen, for toilet things. As carefully instructed, we marked every item of kit capable of being marked, from long-sleeved woollen vests and quite long-legged woollen pants to hammock. Each man was given a wooden marker, carved with his name, for smaller items. Larger items were stencilled, but the stencils must have been made up *ad hoc* from individual letters, for I do not recall possessing a personal one. Metal punches were available to stamp out one's name on boots and suchlike — even on a brass plate let into the cap-box for that purpose.

> There's a far bell ringing
>   At the setting of the sun,
> And a phantom voice is singing
>   Of the great days done.
> There's a far bell ringing,
> And a phantom voice is singing
> Of renown for ever clinging
>   To the great days done.

Amazing that one quotes Newbolt with incomplete irony.

The "Captain" (he was in rank a Commander) of H.M.S. *Ganges* had been that in the boys' days. Not due wholly to his rank or position, he sent before him a sense of apprehension, like the Boss, the headmaster of Seafolde House. Yet I remember nothing more of him than that he was slim and smallish, penetrating and fearless in the discovery of departures from *Ganges* standards of conduct and cleanliness. This is the more strange since I served as his messenger during my last week in *Ganges*, though the title must not be taken to indicate some close Mercury and Jupiter type relation. Rather, a Kafkaesque element persisted — was even enhanced by this entry, finally, into the headquarters of what had ruled and shaped us during our weeks of training. Sitting on a bench outside the Captain's Office was just as boring as the waiting previously endured in other *Ganges* milieus; and though some insight was gained into the methods of the Fates — if only the realization, through a glimpse into the Naval signals system, that they had their essential being elsewhere — one was not a jot the less at their mercy or whim.

It has often been remarked that the frustrations (to say nothing of the dangers) of wartime service are largely purged by after years, leaving in the memory mainly the friendships and funny bits. Anguished tedium; the urging on of that no longer precious commodity, time, to get to a period of being off duty, on leave, the return of peace itself — this formed the ground bass of service life for most. That is not to say that in *Ganges* elements of a pastoral idyll were not present and felt at the time — an equal society of shepherds without selfish worries, cut off from the corruption of cities and courts. For those only masquerading as shepherds there was an added pastoral dimension. One soon learnt to call one's hammock "ammick". It was a Class Leader's job to move his class between the mess and the classroom or gymnasium or wherever: one also soon learnt to shout: "Get fell in outside." (Worth noting that the Navy at this date still marched in fours, so my class fell in in two ranks; had to be ordered to number, and then form fours.) The remarkable range of British accents must have struck every recruit — even me, already acquainted with Lancashire, Yorkshire, Scottish and Kentish speech. The common, the pastoral feature was profanity: relentless swearing was almost universal (though not really experienced in its lowest variety until *Ganges* had been left behind). As put in my "ABC of a Naval Trainee":

F is the adjective near every object,
The chief of desires for both genius and dolt.

I myself had a taste for swearing, possibly formed at school. It may well have been developed in contact with such as Ben Goodman in political days. It survives in conversation, even round committee tables, when some outrageous action or character needs to be condemned. The literary problem of how to indicate the usage remains, despite the leniency about printed expression come into being since I wrote *The Perfect Fool*, where dashes are the order of the day. As to the second line of the distich before quoted, the similar force of feeling was mainly marital now the call-up had reached the near thirty-year-olds, reflected in both the poetry and the popular songs of the time, which looked forward to family happiness as well as lovers being physically united.

I fear I have not given a clear picture of life in *Ganges*. The whole experience must be thought banal by outsiders, even perhaps by the participants, not least because it was so commonplace, especially in comparison with more esoteric situations of war, so that writing about it at all may be considered otiose. Yet that period and place, both with strict limits, startlingly illustrate memory's way with the past. Once, I was master of the topography of *Ganges*: now a few ill-joined features present themselves — the great shed along one side of the parade ground, used for drill when the weather was wet, and always for pay parades (those almost oriental ceremonies where one had to utter — like "Open sesame" — the right formula, while presenting one's cap, so as to receive on its hard, flat surface the prescribed *baksheesh*); the curious covered ways (resembling seaside arcades, and bringing back to me those places where I put pennies in machines in childhood) giving access to the messes on either side; the establishment's own stretch of the Orwell (or was it the Stour?) where nautical training took on slightly more naturalism. Faded, too, the precise sounds: calls on an actual bugle, but mostly heard through the Tannoy, except for "colours"; every day on the parade ground the Marine band playing the R.N. march past, "Heart of Oak", Boyce's indestructible tune, Garrick's words made almost risible by the disasters of the time. Lore from those days has also survived forty years: cleaning windows by rubbing them with crumpled newspapers, say. In the world outside *Ganges*, the real world, the raids on London continued somewhat worse than in my former experience; Rudolf Hess descended on Scotland; H.M.S. *Hood* was sunk.

Training at last culminated in various tests and displays. One was able to make, if required, a bowline on the bight; and say what was looming up if, in fog, one prolonged siren blast was heard, followed by two short ones. There was an individual *viva voce* conducted by a young R.N.V.R. officer. One of his questions, as forecast by our instructor P.O., was to ask for the compass to be boxed from one specified point to another. He was visibly taken aback when I said at once, as one reasonable man to another, that I hadn't learnt the compass. "You haven't learnt it?" "No, sir. It was too difficult. I decided to use the time for other things." In the excellent *Manual of Seamanship*, Volume 1, issued as part of one's kit, the pages under the heading "Hints on Learning and Teaching the Compass" were, as a matter of fact, penetrable by the legal mind, even passages such as:

> The eight predominant points are selected and the sixteen new points are named after them. As the four cardinal points are predominant to the four half-way cardinals, so the eight cardinals and half-cardinals are predominant to the intermediates. Thus the sixteen points required are named after the eight cardinals and half-cardinal points, two after each point (one on each side).

But I could not see that ratiocination would enable one to talk one's way fluently from one point to a distant point: learning by rote seemed required, a thing I was never good at.

In my childhood another show, contemporaneous with "The Battle of Zeebrugge", that promised much but led to fright and tears, was an item at the Blackpool Tower Circus called "The Kicking Mules". Why this should have been so is more mysterious, since no unusual noise was involved beyond the sound of mule-hooves on the ingenious mats of door-mat substance that were laid in sections to the shape of the ring before animal acts came on. That the men who responded to the request for volunteers to ride the mules were stooges did not occur to me: in any case, was I truly concerned about their failing to mount or being bucked off or apparently kicked in the arse as they stood unwittingly about? Perhaps alarm stemmed from the creatures' mere existence: beasts with a will of their own, unmanageable by humans — who nevertheless had bred them, owned them, encouraged them, for the purpose of hurting some fellow humans, entertaining others. But this is interpretation very much after the event: my childhood terror was rooted in my character as a member of that part of mankind not enjoying violence or exercising power, for whom war, therefore, constitutes a particularly poor do.

10   Chatham, Aberdeen, Lee-on-the-Solent

The train takes you where you have to go.

— Alan Ross: "Night-Train Images".

It must not be supposed that my detachment was as great as this account of service life has so far perhaps made it seem. In particular, though my leftism had gone off the boil during the years between Terry Warnock and call-up, I still longed for a *bouleversement* in society, could not imagine peace or prosperity coming any other way. I believed conditions were ripening for change — probably most of the time thought it would be thwarted by English reactionaries, or defeat in war by the Nazis. When the U.S.S.R. was attacked by Germany I found it momentarily impossible to believe that Russia and Britain could be on the same side; probably thought muddle-headedly that this would be the signal at last for Britain to sell out by negotiating a separate peace with the Axis powers. It is highly speculative to try to summarise opinions comprehensively in this way, without reference to personal documents of the time. More or less dense detail would have surrounded such views in actuality, and there would be almost day to day inconsistencies. But good evidence of my state of mind is the memory of my pleased approval of a Government propaganda poster of the day (later criticised as foolishly pointing the "we" and "they" division of English society) — YOUR COURAGE, YOUR CHEERFULNESS, YOUR RESOLUTION, WILL BRING US VICTORY — being amended by someone writing underneath: "Uncle Joe will do it on his tod."

It may need explaining to some today that "Uncle Joe" was a by

150

no means unaffectionate nickname for Stalin, used by more than members of the C.P.G.B. and fellow travellers. The "smiling moustaches" persona lived still. The belief was not eccentric that Hitler, in invading the Soviet Union — that was in the June of 1941 — had at long last bitten off more than he could chew, though the Russian retreats soon seemed to confirm those who all along considered the Russian armed forces on a par of rotten hollowness with its industrial development and political régime.

It must have been June, too, when the cakewalk that so far had been my Naval life came to a suspension by my going from *Ganges* to Chatham Barracks. Every rating in the R.N. has a home base, chosen for him on the basis of domestic convenience, insofar as Chatham, Portsmouth and Devonport can be said to be convenient to other than southerners. Mine was Chatham, so, after end-of-course leave, there I went. I have forgotten the figure of the then current overcrowding, and must not make a guess for fear of underestimation. The discomfort and squalor were sensational. It was said some ratings had been there for many months, overlooked among the thousands of changing names, or (more plausibly) their names removed, by bribery or other means, from the filing system; but it is hard to credit that anyone would want so much to avoid the enemy as live there indefinitely without pay, on barrack rations. What did strike me was the apparently slim chance of being found in this ant-heap for the long course opted for in *Ganges*: much more likely was the forced resumption of my destiny as a C.W. candidate and a draft to a big ship. Indeed, is it a mere chimera of memory that I had actually been on a draft to a cruiser when a metaphorical messenger galloped up with a reprieve? Perhaps a dream.

Mercifully there were three watches at Chatham; Red, White and Blue: that meant two nights out of three could be spent "ashore". In barracks, unless one had a night duty, such as fire-watching, it was compulsory to sleep in the tunnel. Once again, topography has become shadowy. My recollection is that the tunnel or tunnels in the chalk of Chatham's geology were not far from the messes, but this may not have been so, some *via dolorosa* bearing one's ammick possibly involved. Whenever I so spent the night — I think it was not more than three or four occasions — I seem to remember slinging my hammock early in the evening, profiting from the experience of the first occasion. For as the evening wore on the tunnel filled up — the hammocks, eventually swollen with their occupants like the larvae of gigantic bugs, thickly dependent from

151

the tunnel walls — and the farther one had to penetrate the worse the fetid miasma grew, one's nostrils smitten by the odour of thousands of feet and farts. The light provided was dim; to read, even to find hammock fixings, an electric torch was almost indispensible.

No wonder the various servicemen's dosshouses in Chatham were well patronized, it being as advisable to go early and book one's accommodation as a place in the tunnel. I seem to think the price asked was no more than sixpence. The amenities offered were only tolerable in comparison with the tunnel. Each man might have a cabin to himself, but the partition walls would not extend to the ceiling, so one heard every sound from adjoining cabins, including, on a weekend night especially, occasional retching, as well as groans and what in a poem I called the "drummings of fluid on enamel", that being the material of the chamber-pots provided.

It will seem curious to poets now, as it does to me, that I did not exploit more thoroughly the material life then unfolded, having found one reasonably satisfactory way to do it in the poem referred to, called "Saturday Night in a Sailors' Home". This was a simple sonnet in octosyllabics, further democratised by the introduction of a couple of phrases of what was intended as verisimilitudinous speech, e.g. "Please shake me at five" — "shake" being the Navy word for rouse from sleep, therefore in frequent use because of the perpetual business of going on watch. John Lehmann was at that time choosing the poetry for *Tribune*, and I well recall him objecting to the original two phrases as being insufficiently colloquial. I changed and, however unlikely it may seem, improved them: the superfluous "please" had to be kept because it was a rhyme word — no bold Yeatsian changing of rhymes schemes for me in those days, nor for donkeys' years subsequently. What one was after was a Sassoon-like directness, which lack of skill in my case made difficult to combine with the traditional forms that Auden had, after the experimentalism of the Twenties, rendered pretty well obligatory once more. All the same, I am glad *vers libre* was out of fashion, for the task of being a "war poet" (by no means a conscious aim: rather the problem of continuing, in the role of serviceman, to write verse at all) might then have been too easily, superficially achieved. I could say, indeed, that one aspect of a whole lifetime's poetry has been the effort of trying to make strict forms "natural", using that last word to beg a number of more or less complex questions.

As a matter of fact, on reflection, I am sure the poem at issue, if not its nocturnal experience (though the latter must have been renewed in Portsmouth), came from a later time, when creation was more fluent than in those quite early service days, the period at Seafield Park I am going to come to. So what the three weeks or so of Chatham Barracks offered in the early summer of 1941 I failed to poeticize. In retrospect the days seem to have been varied enough to provide modest reader-interest. After breakfast — and here I break off to say that all meals in the Chatham messes were a sad come-down after *Ganges*, parodies of what one had grown used to. It was not so much the quality of the food that was questionable as its volume, temperature and presentation. The great mess buildings must have been built in Edwardian or late Victorian times, resembling the setting for some early Chaplin film of proletarian tenement life, farcical but with cruel undertones (or, more appositely, for a Soviet film about, say, the 1905 Revolution; Eisenstein's masterpiece *Strike* coming to mind — men on balconies, moving up and down staircases, some not in first youth, with bottle-noses or pock-marks, and suchlike images, if not the critical maggots of *Potemkin*). It must have been difficult to prepare the daily muster-rolls for the large, shifting population; and to ensure the availability of reliable "cooks" to fetch and dish out sufficient food promptly from the galley. At breakfast, a small sausage and broken egg might be one's lot; at dinner a not over-generous ladle of stew mainly absorbed by mash.

After breakfast all had to parade for duties to be assigned. I rather think skulking was guarded against by "clear lower deck" being piped, but may be wrong about this since such a drastic order, repeated daily, would surely lose its force in time. My first chore was to chip rust off a frigate preparatory to painting it. Some crude tool was provided, and the anti-rust party sent off in an open truck to the quay where the frigate lay alongside. As the truck proceeded through the dockyard another film sequence was unfolded, this anticipating the Ealing comedies that lay seven years ahead. The civilian employees of the dockyard — the dockyard "mateys" — were successively revealed, singly or in groups, on ships and quays, behind sheds and stores, talking, smoking, meditating, just as though the forces of fascism had already been defeated and an epoch of peaceful leisured prosperity ushered in. Did one see hands of cards being played, as in the articled clerks' room at Wylie Kay's? That may be a slight exaggeration of the emancipated idleness everywhere apparent. It was a surprise that all the men were civilians, presumably exempt from call-up through their (non) occupation.

Continuity in the work assigned was at the mercy of chance. There was only one day of frigate-chipping. On another day I was in a party of ratings taken by coach to the Natural History Museum in South Kensington, which had apparently been used as a temporary Government store for semi-perishable foodstuffs, like dried peas and beans, now required to be removed as museum exhibits, loaded up on trucks and taken to some destination undisclosed to the Chatham hands. Sacks of the victuals were ranged along the extensive corridors, and there was a pong in the air reminiscent of the Chatham tunnel. When the sacks were taken up, mice ran out and nests of young mice were revealed, droppings abounding. I could not participate in the mouse mass murder (fly-stunning days far behind); didn't much like even pulling out the sacks. But it was not too difficult to station oneself away from the noisome action; probably a prefiguration of how one would behave in more lethal Naval encounters. A mid-day meal had been laid on — perhaps merely chits provided — at a services canteen at Westminster. Without being able to communicate any particular detail, I remember emerging that summer afternoon on the pavement opposite the Abbey with a strange sense of semi-freedom, not envying the Londoners going about their business, rather with a virtuous, complacent feeling at having been captured by and made part of the Andrew (after such resistance as had been possible), at being on view in uniform, at working on the disagreeable mission among the pink mouslings and grey mouse-shit of S.W.3. A few *Ganges* friends were still with me — perhaps Flitcroft, whose professionally smart square-rig would in those circumstances rub off on his companions to their advantage. Within sight were the Parliament buildings and civil service offices where all the immense waste and muddle — frigates, man-power, dried peas, japanned hat-boxes — were somehow being pointed in approximately the right direction, and willed to move. But I do not expect I thought then, as I think now, that those sacks of peas were the raw material not only of the vendor who used to cry "Hot peys!" near 208 Hollins Road on Sunday afternoons in my boyhood, but also of Sammy's snack-bar, returning yet again into my life like some symphonic theme, truly living up to the name my grandfather used to give them of "musical fruit".

From Chatham I must have gone up to London, when I was watch off, to see Julian and Kathleen, perhaps fitting in a few frames of snooker, but memory does not particularise — though a sensation comes to me of appearing to old friends for the first time moustacheless, with short hair, and sunburnt glow of health, all the more apparent by the *décolleté* cotton-flannel. I would have been accompanied by service respirator, a far different object to that fitted by Mrs "Y-cwt" in Kennington days, and Navy-issue attaché-case. Did I also take great-coat or oilskins? Either would have been unwieldy in summer, yet at that date I had not bought out of pusser's stores one of the admirable navy-blue belted raincoats (a garment that much later I used as an officer, having removed belt and belt-loops to make it conform with the style prescribed for commissioned level).

A "buzz" had long had it that one of the "W/T" courses one's name was down for would be held in Aberdeen, and that was where the apparently blind and lumbering machine miraculously despatched me to from Chatham, part of a smallish draft of old *Ganges* faces, plus a few other miscellaneous ratings. Was it for that rather long journey that a packed meal was provided for each man, which included what was ineffably called in the Andrew a "tiddy-oggie"? It may have been so, for however slap-dash the individual messes, the galley at Chatham could well have been resourceful enough to make individual meat-and-potato pasties.

I never returned to Chatham Barracks in uniform, for after the course in Aberdeen I was assigned to the Fleet Air Arm, and my base became Lee-on-the-Solent. It was a curious occasion in the mid Seventies that took me back at all. Bernard Miles asked me to join half a coach-load, mainly actors and actresses, going to Chatham to represent the Mermaid Theatre in a ceremony accompanying the handing over of a ship's bell hanging in the theatre foyer in exchange for the new bell of H.M.S. *Mermaid*. The point of the exercise, a typically Milesian blend of publicity, benefaction, and sentiment, was that the theatre's bell was old, coming from the original (or, at any rate, some quite ancient) H.M.S. *Mermaid*, and had hung in the first Mermaid Theatre when that had been in the Miles' back garden. I had known Bernard on and off for years, meeting him first in 1947 when he was one of the readers in a series of radio programmes I did about Stephen Spender. My imitation of his rendering (in the voice later to make famous the virtues of Mackeson's stout) of two phrases from Spender ("Return, return, you warn! We do" and "hot, red walls") had led to their being applied in the family in a variety of wider contexts. Perhaps his interest in the R.N. had started when he played a rating in the film *In Which We Serve*, made in 1942. At the time of his Chatham jaunt I was helping with the Sunday evening "Poetry at the Mermaid" programmes.

Tenuous and strange the memories and emotion of the revenant! A few things at Chatham were recognizable after thirty-five years, or whatever it was — for instance, the main entrance where one was inspected before going ashore; falling-in and surrendering one's watch-card (providing proof one was not duty watch and also a check for the barracks if one went missing). One might, too, be searched for "rabbits", stores being illegally taken ashore. To have one's card removed (by an accomplice on duty there) from its box in the office on the main gate was said to be a wise preliminary to deserting. The Mermaid Theatre party de-coached in front of the pretty eighteenth century house occupied by the Commodore, where we were expected for coffee. This building, and others from the like period, seemed faintly familiar, perhaps glimpsed on the way to the tunnel. Next, the coach took us through the locale of the slothful mateys to the quay where H.M.S. *Mermaid*, a frigate, was berthed — possibly where I had chipped at the earlier frigate. I was glad to see, though never doubting it would be done, the ensuing ceremony carried out by the Andrew in pusser style; precision and the Marine Band moistening the eye. Awnings had been rigged over the deck where the theatre and other guests were seated, bringing back thoughts of that subtle variation of rifle drill, taught in *Ganges* by the anti-cream-puff P.O., for use in tropical waters when awnings prevent the full extension of fixed bayonets. Seats on the quayside, facing the ship, had been provided for the families of the crew, a touch not untypical of the Service, but which I suppose might have been absent before the war. After lunch we looked round, actually being offered drinks in the Chiefs' mess, snug, rather trendy décor. A number of wives were going to Australia, where *Mermaid* was to be based for her forthcoming commission: another bit of human-ization perhaps given a fillip by the influx of Hostilities Only ratings during the war.

But all the latter part of the *Mermaid* outing was seen in tones of rose. After the bell ceremony we went to the Wardroom for lunch. The pre-lunch drink offered seemed champagne, but the shallow glasses had a frosted rim that proved to be sugar. The things were champagne cocktails, generous in brandy, served in a style probably dating back, before Jutland or Zeebrugge, to the

Entente Cordiale, the recipe and procedure preserved somewhere in the Officers' Stewards' manuals. The cold collation that followed was far from the exiguous stew and mash of old Chatham times — though making hardly a greater contrast in that context than the life arrived at in Aberdeen that summer of 1941.

We were the first batch of ratings for the course, to be held in the part of Robert Gordon's College that in peace time was a boys' day school, the boys having been evacuated or merged elsewhere, some of the staff retained or brought back. Or it may have been that the staff came from the polytechnic establishment in the same place. There was little or no evidence of the Navy's presence. Down near the fish market were the offices of the Port Officer i/c (or some such title), a small R.N. organization, already overburdened, dealing with personnel on armed trawlers and the like. It struggled initially to cope with our pay, but little more. We were spread among civilian digs, mine rather good, in the main street though just beyond the main shops. The atmosphere was not far from that of peacetime summers of the past: modest seaside lodgings occupied by respectable but jolly bachelors, pubs and girls in mind. However, the penny soon dropped among the grass widowers that they might up their status, it being theoretically possible to draw a living-out allowance from the Andrew and, thus supported, move to suitable family accommodation. I was a pioneer in making the moves required to outwit the nay-saying bureaucracy, blend of the Kafkaesque and the Schweikian, and eventually I was joined in excellent lodgings, a little farther out towards Hazlehead, by my wife and son: amazing leniency by the Fates.

Though life took on many of the characteristics of ordinary family life (one of the greatest incongruities, indeed, being seen off by Kate in the mornings not to work but school), service friendships went on, flavoursome, essential, as ever. I have failed to find a way to suggest the richness of such friendships (if that is not too grandiose a term for what could often aptly be compared to ships that pass in the night) — particularly omitting accounts of the personalities revealed, for circumstances often gave little chance for relations to develop.

On the Aberdeen course, some of them sharing those initial digs, were men known from *Ganges* days, a few to be known through future time, one or two becoming close friends. Many were Scots, probably chosen by the roughly affectionate Andrew for Aberdeen rather than for the similar courses held simultaneously elsewhere.

In early days re-encounters were multiplied by the premonitory nature of service. Delayed a week or two here and there, one lost some acquaintances, regained others, but the simple design of training imprinted itself quite clearly on the whole mass. Then the Navy was a comparatively small service, inherently amenable to coincidental encounters through the sub-division into home bases — and once in the Fleet Air Arm, a smaller sub-division still, life positively resembled Charles Dickens's schema of repeatedly reintroducing evil or comic characters (indeed, one recalls Dickens's childhood experience of the characteristics of Naval base life at Chatham Dockyard).

Robert Gordon's College consisted mainly of modest buildings round what was a playground rather than a quadrangle. There, a former life was resurrected. One did not quite expect Waller's twitching specs to come through the entrance gates, but — particularly at first, when one's mathematics were put to the question — the Boss seemed nothing like a dozen years away. In a large classroom, seated at desks, the miscellaneousness of the intake was apparent. Though the bulk of it was of recent entry, there were also those who had seen service, a few hard to imagine possessing the required qualifications. There was no fly-stunning and perhaps no fountain-pen thieves, but the atmosphere was more of the Seafolde House fourth form than the fifth. I think all, or almost all, the instructors were from the College: they were excellent. It may be that as in some inflated version of Anstey's *Vice Versa*, they were apprehensive at changing juvenile charges for adults, but they quickly found the required tone, and I guess enjoyed the challenge, certainly in the pioneering days.

Almost at once there was a test, presumably to weed out the hopeless. There may have been some preliminary instruction. For instance, log tables soon appeared. It was as though one had to drive a car after a pedestrian dodecade of years. For a few minutes the apparatus seemed enigmatic; than after a simple enquiry one was away. The few eliminated by the test were augmented by the defection of some not relishing months of what promised to be arduous brain work.

I suppose we were clearly told the scope and purpose of the course, though reliable information in the services was usually preceded by rumour among the lower orders, as in some Shakespearean mob scene before the entry of the lords or tribunes. It was also (if I may yet again educe that writer) akin to what one usually gets in Kafka: knowledge of supreme authority, and of the behaviour it expects, coming from such as ostlers and chambermaids. Moreover, as in Kafka, it was not always clear that supreme authority knew what was wanted, what it was doing even. The Robert Gordon's course began with rapid revision of some mathematics and physics, followed by more detailed study of electricity and wireless, accompanied by practical instruction. All this done, we would go on to a further course in radar at some R.N. establishment. The idea was to create out of the ignorant job lot assembled in Aberdeen and elsewhere a cadre of radar-mechanics, capable of opening up and repairing radar's various boxes of tricks. I do not know that I had any clear notion, even in its simplest terms, of what radar was. Indeed, the term used by the English, if used at all, was not radar but R.D.F. (radio direction finding) or radiolocation. Still, probably some concept of locating and measuring the distance away of objects by bouncing wireless waves off them had been absorbed from popular articles in the press.

As to the theoretical side of the course, no more physics and mathematics were required than the Boss had imparted to me — though that may not be strictly true, for as I write I remember an instructor at Aberdeen using the device of the square root of minus one, which I am sure I had never played with myself, though not ignorant of the concept. The Boss would have loved quietly to acquaint the Fifth Form with it; having no call to carry past the Fourth Form his theatrical — Zulu war-dancing — style of teaching. Possibly the business had not in the Twenties descended to school level; just as I feel our text-books did not grapple with particles smaller than the atom, and that it was after I left school that I read such exciting things as Eddington's semi-popularizations of the (still-called) new physics.

Thinking of this late, Aberdonian vindication of the Boss' emphasis on the scientific side of the curriculum, reminds me that S. H. Birch, in our correspondence following *Souvenirs*, told me that for a reason undisclosed he visited the school in the early Thirties. He went in by the entrance to the School House used by the boys, and in the room by that side door, the boarders' common-room, found the Boss gloomily eating a supper of bread and cheese and pickles, spectacle incredible a few years before. It may have been vacation time, or there may have been no boarding pupils left. The Headmaster's fortunes must have then been near their nadir. The common-room was where the supper cocoa was served, inferior to the *Ganges* brew. Birch reported that the Headmaster was meticulously piling geometrical shapes of bread with cheese and pickle, for convenient consumption — as does Mr Pemberton, the Headmaster of *The Ruined Boys*, with his private supply of toast, butter and marmalade. The common-room is also depicted in that novel: it is where the hero, racked with toothache, reads *Letters from High Latitudes* and is summoned to see Mr Pemberton about his first wrong-minded letter home — a "failure in communication", as the prison governor in the film *Cool Hand Luke* might have called it.

The Headmaster of reality I believe took a humble teaching post after his school expired but, like Freud's obsessional patients, did better with the coming of war, joining and getting on well in the A.R.P. organization, if not the Blackpool counterpart of L. E. Swann. He might have been cheered further had he known how deeply ingrained his teaching was proving to be at Robert Gordon's. The practical work was more exasperating to one who had never in his life filed a piece of metal or soldered a wire. Messing about with some exercise that employed the five-volt, accumulator-fed ring round a laboratory, I once cried out aloud: "I'm too old for this course." I did indeed sometimes feel myself back on the treadmill of study I had sworn after my second spell at Gibson's never to step on again. Yet, as in the case of *Ganges* squad-drill, conscience and application turned most of us — former pen-pushers practically to a man — into passable tradesmen. The splendid technical instructor, to whose lucidity and patience we owed much, was said to be surprised and pleased; though I heard that later, inevitably less creamy, classes did not come up to the standard we set.

I have implied, if not precisely stated, that an insufficiency of irony characterized pretty well all my earlier literary work. This may seem strange in view of the frivolity shown in the present and my previous memoirs. In the latter I mentioned some cod book-titles that had caught my fancy as a boy. In the London Library recently I encountered the philosopher Anthony Quinton, who said he had found *Souvenirs* funny. I asked him if he had liked the book-titles. He said some were familiar; that in past times he had invented a few himself; and only the other day had heard a new one: *The Wild Party* by Segovia Carpet. It is true the unlikely but not impossible forename gives the example high status, but rather typical of me that Quinton's deeper remarks on previous occasions are forgotten and unrecorded in my annals.

When I was a youngish writer it seemed I could only be ironical about things of which I ideologically disapproved — right-wing politicians, say. (Though as I write these words an ironical phrase, surely from early days, comes unbidden to mind: "Submarines like turds that bump around our coasts" — but not as part of an in any way successful poem). This cast of mind, essentially adolescent, accounts for my finding D. H. Lawrence such a sympathetic writer for so long. Since Lawrence is only ironical about obvious villainies or Aunt Sallys he himself has set up — remaining blinkered about charismatic heroes, sexual passion, and so forth — his work is so full of bosh as to become impenetrable (or at least intensely irritating) in maturer years. A good example in my own case is from an unfinished novel of my articled clerk's days, Marston's appearance as a wholly serious character, "Knype" — the very name chosen (incisive, swashbuckling, odd) implying the author's essential approval. This artistic romanticizing of one's life had its counterpart in reality, but on an altogether more modest scale, and diminishing as the years rolled by (though it comes to me that few, if any, of the comic aspects of John Davenport are shown by the character founded on him in my novel *Fantasy and Fugue*). There was no reason why in Aberdeen I shouldn't have written verse (prose fiction, too, for that matter) that kept to the small-scale realism of the situation (like Chekhov and Goncharov) but still captured the dangerously-poised age — no reason except lack of talent.

The few poems that have survived from Aberdeen, meagre sum, are mostly in fairly clotted vein — one, in fact, a versification of themes from Frazer's *Golden Bough*, would not have been out of place in the Fortune Press collection, though its references to war would be taken by the sympathetic reader as having contemporary relevance. Some other pieces bring in natural objects in and around Aberdeen, but without much enterprise; and mention guns and aircraft and other things then much mentioned in everyday life. I was conscious that the sea (so cold all that summer that we never bathed in it, enthusiastic though we were) was the sea my father had seen in his mysterious childhood in Lybster, a town now a mere hundred and fifty miles to the north.

> Where the coast curves the waves' blown smoke
> Blurs with the city's and the pencilled ships
> Lumber like toys. The searchers for coal and driftwood
> Bend; and the beach is littered with stones and leaves,
> Antlers of seaweed, round gulls, to the belt
> Of sand, like macadam, watered by the sea.

Passable as scene-setting, it might be said; but followed merely by a rhetoric and an attempt at generalization that had already been finely brought off by Stephen Spender in the poems that were to be collected in *Ruins and Visions* (1942), later memorably read by Bernard Miles. Any notion of adding family perspectives to such donneés lay even farther in the future.

One Aberdonian piece does reflect the situation (as Terry Warnock would have called it) with reasonable accuracy and sobriety, "Defending the Harbour"; though when I put it in my *Collected Poems* of 1962 I could not forbear to change (apropos my fellow defenders) "the kind and speaking faces" to "the kind and comic faces". Behind the poem lay the Navy's increasing and illogically-resented interference with the lives we were leading of academic days and amatory nights. A petty officer, perhaps a Chief, appeared, to initiate the harbour defence company, pre-class physical jerks, and the church parade before referred to. Nonetheless, existence continued to have strong civilian elements until we left Aberdeen, which incredibly was as late as November 1941, the title given, as a matter of fact, to the poem from which come the six lines I have just quoted.

Pioneering, the course almost inevitably prolonged itself. One of the instructors left to be himself instructed (in a service establishment, or perhaps manufacturer's research department) and returned to communicate, with an excitement shared by most, details of some special radio circuits. Like some bizarre feminine fashion, wavelengths were drastically shortened. The techniques were said to be analogous to those of television, then never even seen as an end-product save by a few thousand set-owners. Did we know why we were studying circuits that produced on the oscilloscope a series of pointed or squarish wave-forms? I think not with any confidence. Since there was no "security" at Aberdeen and the teaching staff were civilians, secret material was not used on the course. The instructor to whom details of the "special circuits" had been imparted was cagey, respected confidences, emanated an air of "I could a tale unfold" had he been free to do so.

These matters impinged on my writing no more than had milk-adulteration case law, or building society statutes, in the past. Even wireless of normal wave-lengths formed no part of our lives, though in our digs we played a portable gramophone actually bought new in Aberdeen. The make was H.M.V., like the radiogram that had gone into store with the rest of our furniture, brand fidelity probably stemming from the corniculate machine owned by my grandparents, perhaps even then still playing Harry Lauder and Luigini, though more likely not, for my grandfather was dead, my grandmother to die soon. The shop that sold us the gramophone also sold us records, good relations being established with a cultivated and obliging lady assistant. The apparatus acquired had half gone out of mind until with a slight shock I read the following stanza-and-a-bit in my son's "Epistle to Bryan Kelly" more than thirty years after:

> My love for tuneful music dates
> From *Figaro* on 78s
> At four or five. When I'm in straits
>   With *Cage* or *Nono*
> I'm glad to know that somewhere waits
>   The *dove sono*.
>
> Or the cool clarinet *con brio*
> In his incomparable Trio . . .

That trio, and the clarinet trio of Brahms that uses a cello instead of a viola, still arouse, if not precise images other than the appropriately navy-blue label Columbia discs bought in Aberdeen, then certainly a sensation of transient felicity not wholly emanating from the music itself.

At last the Hibernian idyll had to end. Farewell to the excellent lecturer whose "er" of hesitation was *in excelsis* the characteristic and imitable Aberdeen "ee", rather saliva-surrounded; to the pubs, unwelcoming to ladies, sometimes confining them with their escorts in waist-high pens, symbolism never quite fathomed; to the delicious species of *croissant*, "buttery rowies", always provided fresh for breakfast by our landlady; to the strong, clean city itself, then supportive of many arts, not least the "varieties", where old favourites were still to be seen. Farewell, above all, to old familiar faces, for at the end of the course some of us were assigned to the Fleet Air Arm, changing our home port to the F.A.A. base at Lee-on-the-Solent. Kate and Johnny and I left Aberdeen together, since I went straight on end-of-course leave. We had to change stations at Glasgow; had time for lunch in some large café, chose haggis from the menu, a good bet in days of even more dubious concoctions. That is all I can bring back of those closing chords, melancholy as Brahms'.

The Royal Naval Air Station, Lee-on-the-Solent (H.M.S. *Daedalus* its pessimistic but not inappropriate cognomen) has become as unfamiliar after forty years as it was initially. There was the main camp and the hutted camp, the latter an addendum, mainly of Nissen huts, occasioned by the war. Naval personnel were slightly diluted by "crabfats", puzzling at first — R.A.F. N.C.O.s, mainly senior, lingering from the days when the Navy lacked its own air arm. Crabfats: I expect at first I was ignorant of the vulgar term, originating in the congruency of the colour of the R.A.F. uniform with that of the ointment prescribed for crab-lice, a specific possibly even then superseded by more sophisticated remedies. Quite quickly one got used to the conjunction of elements: air with water; trainee pilots in square rig, differentiated from Ordinary Seamen and A.B.s by a white cap-band; the strange aircraft still used by the Navy — the Swordfish and the amphibian Walrus strangest — becoming a commonplace, because training, if not operational squadrons, were about in *Daedalus*:

Loud fluttering aircraft slope above his head . . .

Some may have found the second epithet, in that line from the eponymous sonnet of my second book of verse, puzzling or inappropriate; and today even harder to imagine, in the absence of analogous experience, must be a biplane of such cautious landing speed. Mention of uniform is a reminder that this was the moment, alas, when one's own was changed to fore-and-aft rig — an ordinary three-button jacket and trousers, with small-peaked cap. The cries of "Taxi!" with which, after kitting-out at *Ganges*, those dressed as seamen had playfully ridiculed the Writers, could now have been directed at all assembled for the Lee-on-the-Solent radar course, re-rated, for want at the time of a new and more accurate category, "Air Fitters (D.F.)". My glamour had gone, not to be restored until, after years at this dowdy crysalis stage, sudden emergence as R.N.V.R. officer. It was possible to smarten one's appearance in fore-and-aft rig by buying (not from pusser's stores) a tiddley suit, a Number One uniform, made in double-breasted style out of "doeskin", with gold badges. For reasons previously advanced, I never did this; went on suffering the unsatisfactoriness of the issued gear, as years before I had for long suffered the pain of the comedian's Sunday shoes at Seafolde House. One was supposed to fasten all three buttons of the jacket, but this gave a feel (and I suppose a look) of the Jutland or Zeebrugge epoch (though I believe four buttons were regulation then), an effect enhanced by the requirement of returning not just to collar-and-tie but to a collar separate from the shirt, fashion I thought to have liberated myself from for ever more than a decade before, as noted in *Souvenirs*. The Edwardian tone was extended by narrowish trousers, terminating in boots — a look to some degree sanctioned after the war by "Teddy Boy" garb, but then disagreeable to most, if not all. I may say that I had already stopped wearing boots, even my parsimony yielding to the comfort and aestheticism of shoes (allowable, if without toecaps). It was at Lee that both the thrifty and narcissistic sides of my nature were gratified by discovering that for a trifling sum "snobs" (unofficial cobbler) would cut down boots into the simulacra of shoes. I had this done to my better pair of issue boots, and reasonably successful the operation was, though the shoes so formed always needed an effort of will to be worn, if not so great as that required by the comedian's shoes aforementioned.

Come to think of it, I am old enough to have been through the civilian liberation from boots, comparable in emancipatory pleasure with the subsequent liberation from shoelaces. As a very young boy I was photographed in boots, and that was not because, wearing a sailor-suit, I had to submit to naval discipline. I remember my mother referring to shoes as "low shoes"; going into a shop (it would be a few years after the photograph) and saying: "May we see some low shoes, for the boy?" In the days of boots it was a great refinement for them to have metal tabs instead of eyeholes for the last few holes, so that the lace could be slipped round the tab, avoiding the trouble of threading. Tabs also avoided the awkward- ness of getting a knot through the eyeholes: bootlaces always seemed to be breaking. A tab snapping off was a nuisance, however; necessitating an adjustment similar to the effect of a missing tooth. Now, the young often wear a species of plimsoll, but that these are truly liberatory must be doubtful, for they usually lace to the toes, can scarcely be watertight, and possibly lead to smelly feet.

Back under the constant care of the Andrew, duties and delays seemed all the more irksome, though as to the latter there was always the compensation of postponed perils. We were Class Num- ber 1 of trainee radar mechanics in the F.A.A. There was an instruction hut but no equipment; possibly the place had not even been wired up. Some talks on theory were given, of low quality compared with Aberdeen. Two of the lingering R.A.F. Flight Sergeants were involved, I seem to remember, and an R.N. Schoolmaster. When the equipment at last arrived it was decided by Authority that the hut had to be guarded in its unoccupied hours because of its secret contents. The class members formed the guard, on the Wackford Squeers principle. Torture extreme when one got the morning watch (4 am to 8 am), for one slept and was roused in a nearby wooden shed, unlined, ludicrously cold in that severe winter of 1941–42, heated only by one of those odorous oilstoves that cast patterns of light. Probably the middle watch had to sleep there, too. I wore oilskin over greatcoat, despite the struggle to get webbing over that. By then I had the balaclava and roll-neck sweater knitted by a Blackpool knitting group of ladies, centred on Booth's Café, to which my mother belonged. No doubt in the absence of nepotism the articles in question (perhaps knitted by Mrs Spence-Ormerod herself) would have been in use on more serious naval occasions, such as the Murmansk run.

By the D.F. Nissen hut was a brick-built air-raid shelter, unused at night, in the entrance to which it was fairly safe for the guard on duty to skulk at times and have a few drags at a cigarette. As to the last, it would almost certainly be made from a tin of "Ticklers", the duty-free, Navy issue tobacco. Few rolled cigarettes entirely by hand (it may have been otherwise in the earlier war, whence Arthur Pickup probably derived his skill). Common was a little machine still to be seen today, consisting essentially of a pair of rollers with between them what looked like legendary dirty mackintosh. There was another gadget, that ingeniously, if more temperamentally, stuffed the tobacco into paper cylinders, but I never possessed one of those. The lb tins of Ticklers could be had either as cigarette or pipe tobacco: occasionally, the former, more popular, was unavailable, and some made cigarettes from pipe tobacco, but they were a stern smoke. In large establishments it was possible to have your Ticklers converted — on the semi-official "snobs" or Lenin New Economic Policy lines — by a more sophisticated machine into a fair imitation of "tailor-mades", as factory cigarettes were called. "Pricks" of tobacco (the vulgarism for "periques" was apt) were still occasionally procurable, the product within the rope-binding like the "twist" I used to see smoked on Oldham trams in my boyhood, slices for the pipe needing to be pared off with a penknife from the liquorice-like lump.

The anxieties and devoted industriousness arising out of the tobacco issue (there were similar obsessional characteristics attached to the rum issue) illustrated well the trait that causes humans to

166

care more about trivialities than great questions, and which has such spectacular effects when, for instance, the drives and sanctions of religion are removed. The dockyard-matey syndrome, it might be termed: indolence in the very arena, almost, of death and survival — the indolence not, of course, extending to activities such as card-playing and tea-brewing. The thing is so widespread we may wonder how mankind is driven to such serious and deleterious activities as warfare; but humans are not (unfortunately, on the whole, it may be said) dockyard-mateys to the core.

No enemy agent ever turned up to penetrate the secrets of the D.F. hut. I have the feeling the guard was never issued with ammunition, but I could be wrong about this. There is a joke, which I am sure I am not giving the full point of, about the nervous guard who, taught the challenge "Who goes there, friend or foe?" and the ensuing "Advance, friend, and be recognized", on getting the response "Foe", said "Advance, foe." There was this touch of the Fred Karno about the D.F. hut guard, but if that were the reason for its eventually being quietly dropped, a great many service activities merited dropping also. The experience left its mark: pictures return — of reading or trying to read in a camp-bed in the arctic guards' shed (antarctic, rather, for the ambience seemed much akin to that created by Captain Scott, himself R.N.), only trousers and boots removed, the sole light the pattern of beams from the oilstove.

A constant of service life was shortage of reading material. Sometimes I come across a book on my shelves with Lee-on-Solent and the date under my signature. Such a one would probably have been bought at a quite good secondhand shop in Fareham, a town I usually went to in preference to Portsmouth when I went "ashore", but that source did not satisfy all need. In any case, thrift usually dictated that books bought should primarily be lasting rather than readable — readable in the context of Tannoy music or conditions Captain Oates walked out of, any way. Yet even at that time (and times thereafter, in fact) I misjudged what I would have found readable, prolonged hangover from the days at school when I preferred Ian Hay to O. Henry. Would I have tackled Walter Scott's Journal in the hutted camp? I doubt it, though was recently held by it with ostensibly more attractive things available. What a bonus that intellectual development never ceases, in the ill-educated at least!

The year turned, the course proceeded in wandering steps and slow. Authority and insight into the business were eventually brought by the young Sub-Lieutenant Gleave, who had worked for Pye and just been commissioned into the R.N.V.R. especially to instruct in the function and maintenance of the Pye-made A.S.V. sets. The initials stood for Air Sea Vision: the apparatus, installed in aircraft, enabled targets to be distance-measured, and homed on. The display on the miniature cathode ray tube was a vertical line (measuring distance) on which the target showed as a "blip", a horizontal extension on either side of the vertical line. If the aircraft were navigated so as to equalize the extent of the blip about the vertical, it would *ipso facto* be oriented towards the target.

When I let fall I intended to mention A.S.V. in these pages, my wife was discouraging, saying with truth that what was interesting were people not things, particularly things like radar sets. Yet for some reason scarcely to be uncovered, unless it was the tedium in returning to discipline in a large establishment, details of faces, characters and incidents have largely dropped from my memory of those months. What I summon up is the mess, a Nissen hut, of course, filled with double decker beds, uncommodious ablutions by the entrance, an obsession with getting heat out of the coke-burning stoves (illegal raids being organized on the camp's coke-piles), and my actually surreptitiously but vainly examining the leads to the loudspeaker for the possibility of arranging a breakdown to give respite from the musical slush, non-stop save for the recorded bugle-calls, requests for individuals to report to the R.P.O.'s office, and the like. Membership of the mess was not drawn exclusively from the largely middle-class members of the radar class, though the working-class would be principally from its skilled echelon, the main body represented by a few Air Mechanics. Of course, these subtleties were not taken account of by the living conditions provided by Authority, which assumed a fairly low proletarian off-duty life.

I still felt, to use Wilfred Owen's phrase, sympathy for the oppressed, often considered myself one of them; and despite turns of revulsion and exasperation this sense continued until the later conditions of my service life made it irrelevant or dormant. Rage would choke me at being wakened by the thoughtless drunks coming late into the mess after an evening ashore, yet at the same time I could write, with sincerity and self-identification, such stanzas as:

Here in the mess, on beds, on benches, fall
The blue serge limbs in shapes fantastical:
The photographs of girls are on the wall

And the songs of the minute walk into our ears;
Behind the easy words are difficult tears:
The pain which stabs is dragged out over years.

I see that I was absurdly lenient to the Tannoy music: such poetic soft-pedalling helped to give the Service poetry of the Second World War its pervasive sadness and nostalgia, to choose the two qualities I emphasized when criticising it at a later date. However, I had forgotten about, and was glad to find, copying out the lines, mention of benches, so characteristic of naval mess-decks, useful (if not the last word in comfort) for card and ludo players, letter-writers, make-do-and-menders, even readers. But some features of those A.S.V. sets come back with as much particularity as the humans: valves like little pillar-boxes, whose pins, unlike the points of the compass, it was essential to get by heart; or the peculiar awkwardness, due to the interior polythene and the exterior metal braid, of fixing a plug to the co-axial aerial. As to the clip supposed to stop the aerial plug working loose from the aerial socket, this remained a British finger-nipper until American equipment came at a later date to prove their greater regard for comfort even of radar mechanics.

11 Seafield Park

The courteous reader will scarcely fail to observe that these pages abound with such parenthetical expressions as "I think", "I fancy", "I imagine", "I should say", "If I remember aright", "If my memory serves me correctly", "To the best of my knowledge", and so forth. These parentheses will not, perhaps, weary or exasperate my readers quite beyond endurance, when I tell them that the "thinks", "believes", etc, have been inserted purely for conscience' sake.

— George Augustus Sala: Things I Have Seen and People I Have Known

---

I related in *Souvenirs* how, after writing (but before publishing) *The Ruined Boys*, I found that my old headmaster, the "Boss", whose persona had suggested my fictional headmaster, C. Howard Pemberton, was still alive. I had intended calling my fictional school Seafield House, but in the light of my near-disaster with the Boss, checked with the famous "scholastic agents" Gabbitas, Thring and Co Ltd, also asking them if they knew of any schoolmaster with a name similar to the one I had invented. They replied with polite efficiency.

16th August, 1957

Dear Sir,

Thank you for your letter of August 13th. We are interested to hear about your novel concerning Seafield House.

The nearest name to this was a school, Seafield Park at Fareham in Hampshire, which closed down some years ago, although the tradition of the school has been carried on under another name. The present school is known as Newells, near Horsham, Sussex.

There is also a school known as Seafield at Bexhill-on-Sea. This is also a fairly old-established school and is a very flourishing one.

The nearest approach to your Headmaster is a master called Christopher Henry Pemberton, who we believe is an assistant master at Shrewsbury School.

We have had to look up our old records, which go back as far as the 1870s. Some of them are not in perfect condition and we cannot, therefore, guarantee that there have not been Headmasters called C. Howard Pemberton.

The above information has resulted from a certain amount of research work, and we think that a fee of two guineas would be reasonable.

Yours faithfully,
Gabbitas Thring.

Of course, I had indicated that my enquiry was a professional one, and gladly sent the modest sum asked, at the same time enquiring further if their records showed any school called "Seafolde House". They replied in the negative, and wished the book "great success" — in vain.

"Seafolde" was invented more or less on the spur of the moment, its touch of the archaic calculated to remove it, as Gabbitas Thring confirmed, from the possible. I was nervous of retaining "Seafield House", in view of the Bexhill-on-Sea "Seafield", which, however old-established and flourishing, might have have imagined itself defamed by my account of the fictional school.

Gabbitas Thring's mention of "Seafield Park at Fareham in Hampshire" gave me a frisson of surprise, though not in the same class as Guy Crouchback's experience with the Electronic Personnel Selector in *Unconditional Surrender*. I knew Seafield Park. Moreover, it had provided some of the topographical features of the school in *The Ruined Boys*, and prompted my choice of the original name "Seafield House". Seafield Park was, in fact, at the time of my acquaintance with it, an overflow establishment for R.N.A.S., Lee-on-the-Solent. I realize only too well that I may already have lost the attention and comprehension of readers with less interest

171

in the business than I: the ensuing tabulation is intended to elucidate the nomenclature situation (the current cliché word is surely justified) that finally resulted.

The following interlocking actualities and concepts emerged:
(1) The real school of my schooldays, which in the present book and in *Souvenirs* I have called Seafolde House. Since this was not, of course, its actual name, in the discussion that follows I shall designate it "Seafolde House", the inverted commas differentiating it from the fictional school of the next heading.
(2) The invented school of *The Ruined Boys* (published in the United States as *That Distant Afternoon*) also called Seafolde House, which I shall refer to without inverted commas.
(3) The real school, subsequently (and as I knew it) the naval establishment near Fareham, in truth (and here) called Seafield Park.

I fear, as I see having set it out, that this I. A. Richardsesque apparatus may confuse even the reader who has conscientiously persisted thus far, but possibly some residual uncertainty is not inappropriate in questions of memory, invention and reality.

I do not know at what date boys and masters had left Seafield Park, but when I went there in March 1942 there were signs still of its former function — not merely in the miscellaneousness of its buildings, reflecting the processes of growth and decay so characteristic of prep schools and the like, blossoming in ambitious but institutionalized décor such as timber panelling — seen also in more stable organizations like the Equitable — but also notice and honours boards; well-used upholstered furniture in which might be imagined pipe-smoking beaks of not very far-off days.

Seafield Park was seemingly restored to scholastic use after the war (though Gabbitas Thring did not imply this with certainty) but presumably failed to survive the perils of the ensuing period, such as the Butlerian improvements in free education, or possibly the proprietor's demise. In taking some of its physical features in order to disguise "Seafolde House" and lessen the risk of defamation claims, I did not make the fall of Seafolde House less intrinsically improbable. But I thereby almost inevitably upgraded the status of Seafolde House (compared with that of "Seafolde House"), not least by setting it near a small sea-side resort rather than more or less in the middle of a big one. "Seafolde House" is described in *Souvenirs*: a pair of large semi-detached houses in a street of such, with playground and one-storey classrooms at the rear. The fictional

Seafolde House and the actual Seafield Park were set in grounds of their own, conforming much more to the traditional notion of the middle-class prep school. The Boss having to teach and instil moral values in an ambience far less agreeable and calcitrant than that of Seafolde House makes him a worthier figure than C. Howard Pemberton, so it is just, after all, that the spartan fare and doleful dumps observed by S. H. Birch in the early Thirties was eventually succeeded by better things.

Writing the word "spartan' brings to mind an aspect of the Boss not hitherto revealed: his classicism. The three, wholly notional "Houses" among which the school population was divided were called Trojans, Titans and Spartans, and there were other links between the school and the ancient world. When I mentioned the three watches at Chatham Barracks, Red, White and Blue, it came back to me that colours were also attached to the three school houses. I was a Spartan, with the unusual colour (blue and red being assigned to the other houses) brown. On Sports Day, and perhaps for house soccer matches, one had to wear shorts of house colour. On a wet afternoon one Spartan boy's shorts, thriftily dyed by his mother, "ran", giving an unfortunate effect down his legs. I forget the boy's identity. Not the Spartan I best remember, Foreshew, whose presence on my side in house cricket matches I thought of as another instance of my luck in life.

I do not know whether the Boss conferred or merely inherited the house titles, but despite mathematics and science being his chief concerns he was not above taking a class in Latin. Myself, I dropped Latin at an early age, but his teaching of it was as effective as his other intimations to the puerile mind. He probably inherited the school motto, *Labor omnia vincit* (under a crest, one of the quarterings of which was a seaside pier — presumably representing, as nearer the school, the pier that displayed the talents of Fred Walmsley rather than the one where I used to see John Davenport's mother), but there were Latin tags over the sections of "Form Notes" in the school magazine which I fancy may have stemmed from the Boss. How straitened, really, one's knowledge of his character! I made C. Howard Pemberton something of a hypocrite; and the school magazines of "Seafolde House" do contain phrases and attitudes, of Pecksniffian kind, that surely had the Boss' blessing if not his authorship. Yet now I would hesitate before condemning or ridiculing the call, the aspiration, to virtue, in whatever dubious terms it expressed itself. In a lifetime of almost seventy years the question of shifts — even of cycles! — in morals must arise, both in oneself and the world. The business seems crucial when, as today, freedoms sought have been achieved without the accompanying sanctions once thought essential. But perhaps it is ever thus as old age looks back.

When John Lehmann showed me the typescript of his book *Rupert Brooke: His Life and Legend* (1980), I mildly objected to his pretty well wholesale condemnation of the sonnet sequence "1914". I had come to think that those poems not despicably, if vaguely, impugn unserious love and selfish life (to put it banally), and express hope for a future society of true comradeship. Of course, especially in the light of conditions on the Western Front, and the immediately ensuing pacifism of Sassoon and Owen, the notion that such a thing could come directly through war and patriotism will never do. All the same, both 1914 and 1939 had certain saving graces in terms of human relations. Being called up in the second affair gave me a strong sense of *déja vu*, expressed in several of the poems which at last, at Seafield Park, I started to write (though in extremely modest numbers) about my shared predicament.

I interpolate here an odd item that seems relevant. The "autograph album", referred to in *Souvenirs*, that my grandparents gave me at Christmas 1917, has an entry in it by my father's friend I. L. ("Issy") Gotliffe, dated 17 January 1918, which quotes the following lines from Kipling's "For all we have and are: 1914":

> No easy hope or lies
> Shall bring us to our goal,
> But iron sacrifice
> Of body, will, and soul.
> There is but one task for all —
> One life for each to give.
> What stands if Freedom fall?
> Who dies if England live?

In the album the quotation is not quite accurate, so it was probably written down from memory. Evidently its sentiments, even at that late date, did not seem absurd to Issy, who was with the B.E.F. in France — though being part of what I imagine was the Red Cross bureaucracy may have preserved his 1914-type ideals.

I sent practically all the Seafield Park poems to John Lehmann, finding a sympathy and encouragement that did not exclude critical comment very much apropos. After he had given up the literary editorship of *Tribune* (which was in this Spring of 1942), he considered the poems for *Penguin New Writing*, passing on one or two surplus to requirements to J. R. Ackerley at *The Listener*. In the second volume of his autobiography, *I Am My Brother*, John actually quotes a poem from Seafield Park in which, as happened, the chaplain comes among naval ratings and speaks of moral matters, to their incomprehension — his concepts of "freedom", "good" and "duty" alien to them in their situation. John's comments on the poem, which follow, are perceptive in a way that now touches me greatly, yet I wonder if I thought at the time (still applying a Warnockian rigour to abstract concepts) I was expressing anything more than a Marxist scepticism.

I rather think one didn't get sent from *Daedalus* to Seafield Park (not awfully far apart) unless waiting to be drafted or otherwise a completely "gash hand". At the end of the radar course — it came eventually to an end — I failed, with a few others, the practical test, and had to stay on for a further week's revision. I was never really any good on the practical side of radar, perhaps too frightened by the lurking presence of 4,000 volts or, more likely, lacking an instinct that allied brain and body, evidenced by my cricket, never learning to play a musical instrument, and (according to my wife) not being able to dance well (though my impressions of soft-shoe and ballet dancers have always seemed to me quite effective). A fellow failure was Willie Robertson who had been at Aberdeen but whom I got to know much better during that extra week. He too came to Seafield Park when we had passed a further practical, and had duly been rated up to "Leading Air Fitter (D.F.)", and probably had had end of course leave. More of him anon.

I see myself among the hands at Seafield Park getting fell in in the mornings for duties to be assigned. I doubt there were nearly enough jobs to go round, even on the Services' labour-intensive system, the unemployment problem aggravated by leading hands being too thick on the ground, deemed to be above utterly menial tasks like shovelling coke, though I am not certain that this proposition was always adhered to. Seafield Park was commanded by a commissioned Warrant Officer, called back into the R.N. after retirement, promoted to Lieutenant-Commander; quite an elderly man by service standards. It would seem hardly likely to have been his motor-car I helped to paint (I think not actually applying the colour, but preparing the surfaces, in which the Chatham rust-chipping experience proved its value). Working on his boat, tied up in a nearby creek, is a task I can be more sure about, though never assigned to it: it was reported a soft option, providing bonuses of cups of tea, even food, from the C.O.'s wife. Nor was I ever given the more dubious job of looking after his monkeys, I think two in number. Whether this was mere guard duty, perhaps including mucking them out, or called for skill in grooming or amusing the pets, again memory fails to reveal.

Such daily duties, so redolent of the preoccupations and eccentricities of those in authority, were again reminiscent of school. Where we fell in was cobbled or partly so, former arena of play for the boys of Seafield Park, and before that, in the premises' private house days, maybe forming an approach or forecourt to the stabling. A drive led through paddocks or former playing fields to a road running parallel to the sea, and so to the then sketchy attractions, as a resort, of Lee, configurations that I drew on for *The Ruined Boys*.

I wrote a few poems in a former common-room, quite comfortable in a shabby way, and I fancy not subject to the tyranny of records or radio programmes relayed from the centre. Outside the window was a garden or former garden. Music may well have come from a radio controlled by the common-room's users, and thus occasionally classical, if only on account of inertia. This place was the scene of an unfinished poem found recently in a tiny notebook of the time, of which I quote the opening three stanzas, apparently in their first draft:

> In times of parting drums are powerful,
> The probing restless music tears a skin
> From that already raw, sad sensitivity.
>
> And on the floor I see a brilliant square
> With shapes of trees appearing in it and, as though
> It were the drying of a stain, then vanishing.
>
> And should I go outside, across the furrows
> Shadows will be flying with the April clouds
> And all the fields struck into points of light like gems.

Once more, one is gravelled to know why this not wholly impossible start was abandoned — why in general the work of this Spring of 1942, evidently a time of a certain openness to experience, and decision about form and tone, was not more ample, more worked-on. Physical circumstances might have been more auspicious, but unlike Terry Warnock's job with the Gas Department the chores of Seafield Park could not have absorbed much energy. The poems' dominating theme was separation; a characteristic, indeed, as already noted, of far too much of the verse of the Second World War, particularly in domestic and backward-looking circumstances (though this objection, which even a guilty party like myself held strongly, had to be modified when, after the war, Keith Douglas's collected poems appeared, and later still when Alan Ross collected his revised war poems in *Open Sea*).

When I got to Seafield Park, delay in facing the shooting war — whether deliberate, as in taking up radar at all, or accidental, as by failing the practical — could not be much prolonged, for I was already, or very soon to be, booked for a draft to Ceylon. Nevertheless, I arranged for Kate and Johnny to come down from Blackpool, and stay nearby. I may well have been influenced in this by the comparatively relaxed atmosphere at the overflow establishment, the general sense that manning overseas air bases and the like had to take second place to simian needs, and also by the conviction (sometimes justified, sometimes not) that the wheels of the Andrew ground exceeding slow. I booked a hotel room in Lee for a night or two, before finding excellent digs nearer Seafield Park. The hotel, scarcely to be dignified by the name, was notable in a series we experienced of more or less scruffy places open for business in wartime; memorable chiefly because the first night the only vacant room was on the ground floor, at the door of which, at intervals during the night, there snuffled and scratched, trying to get at us, what proved to be merely an alsatian dog. It was no consolation to learn that it was simply, like us, seeking a night's rest, the room normally where its bedding was. My son, patient and uncomplaining as ever, was below par with a heavy cold and ulcerated mouth. Yet the exercise seemed worthwhile.

It turned out we had no more than a week together. The news that the Ceylon draft was to depart from Seafield Park the following morning came on a day when I was duty watch, so Willie Robertson offered to go to the digs and tell Kate. No better messenger could have been found. Though tall, well-made, excellent at tennis and badminton, and fond of a dram, he was a man of supreme uxoriousness and domesticity. And he lacked the usual disadvantage of messengers, that of being themselves unaffected by their bad tidings,

177

for he, too, was on the Ceylon draft. The next morning Kate enterprisingly borrowed a bicycle from one of our two landladies, and rode to Seafield Park in the hope of seeing me — which she did from a distance over the tail of a truck taking the draft and its bags and ammicks to R.N.A.S., Lee, to join those on the draft already there. There was some arrangement that we might meet later in the day at the British Restaurant in Lee, but the draft was mustered with disagreeable rapidity. The British Restaurant (on the whole one of the ghastlier wartime improvisations, possibly later making its mark on Orwell's *Nineteen Eighty-Four*) had been established in the Tower, a modest municipal pleasure-dome, which I passed in another truck the same morning on the way to the troop train, wondering if Kate and Johnny were within, toying with the vegetable pie.

Looking back from this point, when my life might fairly easily soon have ended, I speculate about strands missed — less, perhaps, in my own life than its relation with the worlds of others. Did he never ponder on *that* public event (we sometimes ask of a collection of a littérateur's letters), never say *this* to his friend? Alas, all too much here confirms a self-centred character, turning to lyric poetry because of the comparative ease of using there the disparate impressions, those "wisps of themes" referred to at the start of *Souvenirs*, in the absence of the genius required to order "perfection of the life or of the work", to put the question in appropriate high falutin Yeatsian terms. I think that writing of post-childhood life may almost inevitably, for various reasons, not least increasing cares, seem to indicate an imaginative narrowing from what had gone before, but I doubt I felt this in actuality. Creativity may have seemed tenuous through Blackpool, Ashford, Blackheath and early R.N. days, but it bucked up a bit in Africa, and then, after a post-war reaction, flourished in several ways down to the present. Not that a writer is at all reliable as to the value of his various "periods".

At Seafield Park I was "En l'an trentiesme de mon eage." The epoch that has since elapsed, as I write this, from Seafield Park time is far, far longer than the epoch that at Seafield Park separated me from the events of childhood. No wonder the way old men forget, and remember. Just as vivid in my mind as anything at Seafield Park is the recollection of a horse falling in Copster Hill Road, near my grandparents' house when I was staying with them as a boy. It had been drawing a milk-float. Great efforts were made to get it to its feet. The float was uncoupled; still the horse did not rise. A quite long business ensued, not all of which I watched, probably not relishing what I saw, though at the same time fascinated by another being's ordeal — as, for instance, one may read of Freud's cancer, the harrowing details of which are now available to all, notably from the marvellous book by Max Schur, *Freud Living and Dying*. The shafts of the float pointed upwards, neatly lined with a painted decoration: the horse's occasional struggles seemed frustrated less by injury than some inherent equine propensity to stay down when down. Rain had started falling, as so often in Oldham: the horse was covered by a tarpaulin; and at length carted away, presumably dead, for I recall the lolling of its curiously thick tongue.

My grandfather would sometimes feign to wipe a drop off the end of a grandchild's nose, getting rid of the supposed moisture from his fingers by shaking them in a manner that produced a crack, as of a whip. In later life I divined how he contrived this noise — by holding a finger or fingers rigid, and allow the others to strike against it or them. Not that I could ever effectively do it (indeed, the operation may only have been possible for one with fingers affected by Dupuytrin's Contracture, as were my grandfather's), though sometimes going through the motions with various cousins, my son, and finally my grandchildren. A pity I never got the knack. That must be put in the snooker category.

A verbal memory, equally vivid, was revived by one of the school magazines sent by Stanley Birch. This came out of an account of an excursion by the Photographic Society "in the neighbourhood of Warton and Freckleton". The contribution was unsigned, but I know from internal evidence that the author was the Geography master, already one of my *dramatis personae*, W. S. Groveham Proctor, "Cherry Nose", as appropriately nicknamed. The style is at once formal and idiosyncratic. It would be too much of an imposition to reproduce the item in full, for interest cannot be expected from those not on the excursion. We apparently took the tram car to Lytham, home of Uncle Fred, Auntie Vi, and Harry Clifton, and then "continued on foot along the bank of the Ribble".

A keen east wind, the full force of which was experienced on the riverside, prevented successful photography until a more sheltered locality was reached. Nevertheless, the time was pleasantly spent in negotiating the somewhat difficult obstacles that were encountered in the shape of fences and hedges.

The complete lack of irony, though seeming to be demanded, recalls an aspect of the Upward trilogy already mentioned, *The Spiral Ascent*. One imagines Mr Proctor's nose in that wind, perhaps forbidding irony. But (typical of memory's unreliability, even in recent matters) I see with the texts in front of me that the phrase sought is not in this account of the trip along the River Ribble but in an article in an earlier number of the magazine Stanley supplied, a report headed "The Camera Club's Trip to Pilling" — an expedition to the river on the northern boundary of the Fylde, the Wyre (the Ribble forming the region's southern extremity). The report in this instance was actually signed "W.S.G.P." It began with characteristic climatic doubts, but eventually had to record that the weather turned out to be "ideal": films were exposed and, equally important, the contents of "refreshment baskets" consumed. (What had been put up for boarders, I wonder? Nothing so welcome as would have been tiddy oggies, I guess). And then — here come the reverberant words:

> The hour of our departure arrived too soon for most of us, but it was a happy band that eventually marched towards Knott End to the soothing strains of "Minnetonka", sung by the boys.

Sung by me, I expect, yet I cannot remember the song. Moreover, in my mind the immortal phrase was "the *haunting* strains of 'Minnetonka'." Of course, "soothing" is better, not only adding to the alliterative effect at the end of the sentence but also suggesting the healing of the day's abrasions (for there must have been some, despite the good weather, possibly to do with the refreshment baskets or increasing weariness). "Sung by the boys" seems to me also an inspired touch, alliterative again, with the right dying fall, and reassuring the Boss, the parents, and anyone else of authority whose eyes might fall on the magazine, that even on a Camera Club trip there was no loss of pedagogical dignity.

Thus once again is illustrated the contradiction of memory by the documents of history. One would like to think at least the fundamentals of a poet's prose autobiography were truthfully caught in his verse, but that too is an illusion, as has been shown.

Appendix
(see page 129)

BLACKHEATH: SEPTEMBER 1939

Nights soften as I walk over the common,
Though trees and grass come out a sharper green
In the last misty light. The yellow houses
On the still water are reversed and clean.
But the swan that curved in peace-time has departed.
Into the base of the penumbra lean
The shoulders of summer and our birds and flowers
Fly off to Cancer where shadows are unseen.

I imagine walking for ever in this city
With animals' ghosts and memories of love.
But silent also with the vibrant dove
Are nation after illusion-clutching nation.
And vanished in a day of proclamation,
A decade of profound and useless pity.

THE PHONEY WAR

Sitting at home and reading Julien Benda;
Evening descending in successive gauzes —
Pantomime transformation scene reversed;
A point releasing Haydn from a grove
In waves alternately severe and tender:

A curious way to spend a night of war!

Though more and more clearly I see my bona-fides.
Under the growing pressure of the mould
I'm now compact, one of the very small
And disillusioned poets of the era;
Soothsayers who lived on into the Ides.

So action or avowal would be pretence.
Not that I now may draw back from the edge —
The threat of being pushed into real life
(Or realer death) — or even want to. Nor
Deny the times' need for handbooks of defiance.

182

Is it a lack or growth, this emollient lotion
Of words that keeps me sitting through the dusk,
To find in the martins' squeaking something sure
But vague to praise? This Frenchman says that war
Intensifies the craving for emotion.

He may be right. My own, however, shows
As an increasing fondness for Henry James;
And, if I crave at all, I crave that blight
Shall crumple less millions than thought possible,
And that on those I love shall fall few blows.

A curious war to bequeath me such a night!

BATTERSEA: AFTER DUNKIRK, JUNE 3, 1940

Smoke corrugated on the steel-blue sky
From the red funnels of the power-station
Is blanched as the shocking bandages one sees
On soldiers in the halted train. Patience!
Still there is nothing definite to say —
Or do, except to watch disintegration,
The rightness of the previous diagnosis,
And guard oneself from pity and isolation.

The generator's titanic vessel floats
Beside the Thames; and smoke continues to pour.
Khaki and white move on as though to hide
In summer. What can keep the autumn fates
From breaking the perfect sky and sending power
For slaves to set against the pyramid?

FIRST AIR RAIDS

Not the moon's light —
Theatrical mauve,
Antiquing the city —
Nor winging danger
Nor guns in the grove,
Strange in the night,
Add beauty to anger;

But my undismayed
Pouring of love
In the crouching city
While things more certain
Than Hamlet's glove
Round reckless blade
Strike through the curtain.

Only when that dies
In sewers and streets
Will guns in the city
Fade with history;
Since love completes
Fear and is cries
For what can't be.

LONDON AIR-RAID, 1940

An ambulance bell rings in the dark among
The rasp of guns, and abstract wrong is brought
Straight to my riveted thought.

Tonight humanity is trapped in evil
Persuasive as plague or devil; hopelessly wages
With pain, like the Middle Ages.

My reading and the alimentary city
Freeze: crouching fear and licking pity's all
Of the handed animal.

EPITAPH FOR JAMES JOYCE
January 13, 1941

Reader do not stop to pity
This citizen without a city.
In the grave those eyes will get
No deeper darkness, and the heart
There enjoys perspectives that
Failed in his diurnal art.

INVASION BARGES IN THE CLYDE, 1943

Like new growth pushing through dead stalks —
Barges cocooned in girders in the yard.
These are the hearses for a generation,
Impersonal as a fatal card.

Over the little houses goes,
Like silk released, a flight of foam-white gulls,
While the indifferent workers clang and weld
The soon-to-be historic hulls.

Far off, those birds fall on the waves
Where rock preceded, will outdistance, man:
Their cries, the spray, the sea-black stone proclaim
Absence of destiny or plan.

Who can help weighing loneliness
And chaos against the town's precarious order?
Life after life inexorably flies
From off the system's whirling border.

Over a haunting formless sky
Barges and men eventually will move,
Saved only from constituent dust and ore
By history's spiral, luck's last groove.

121 28

ST. HELENS BOROUGH COUNCIL
LOCAL HISTORY LIBRARY

82131

NOT TO BE TAKEN AWAY